I0109463

Enactments

EDITED BY

RICHARD SCHECHNER

To perform is to imagine, represent, live and enact present circumstances, past events and future possibilities. Performance takes place across a very broad range of venues from city streets to the countryside, in theatres and in offices, on battlefields and in hospital operating rooms. The genres of performance are many, from the arts to the myriad performances of everyday life, from courtrooms to legislative chambers, from theatres to wars to circuses.

ENACTMENTS encompasses performance in as many of its aspects and realities as there are authors able to write about them.

ENACTMENTS includes active scholarship, readable thought and engaged analysis across the broad spectrum of performance studies.

Sylvia Molloy

Crossings

VARIED IMAGINATION
and
LIVING BETWEEN LANGUAGES

EDITED BY

Diana Taylor

Seagull
BOOKS

LONDON NEW YORK CALCUTTA

Seagull Books, 2025

First published in volume form by Seagull Books, 2025
Copyright © Emily Geiger, 2025

Cover design: Sunandini Banerjee, Seagull Books
Cover images: Alice Attie, image courtesy the artist; and rawpixel.com

Hardback ISBN 978 1 80309 519 6

Paperback ISBN 978 1 80309 520 2

British Library Cataloguing-in-Publication Data
A catalogue record for this book is available from the British Library

Typeset by Seagull Books, Calcutta, India
Printed and bound in the USA by Integrated Books International

Para Geiger

CONTENTS

EDITOR'S PREFACE

Diana Taylor

Sylvia Molloy's *Crossings* explores the difficult, disorienting, compelling, and necessary states of living between languages, places, and cultures. Molloy (1938–2022) was a trailblazing Argentine writer and educator, well known for both her fiction and her scholarly writing and teaching about Latin American literature, queer theory, and autobiography. She lived in cities such as Buenos Aires, New York, and Paris without ever leaving the others behind. Fluent in Spanish, English, and French, she inhabited all three languages, shuttling back, forth, and in between, aware that each place, each language brings forth a different self, another vantage point for apprehending the world, an altered path to memory. Living between those places and languages required constant crossing: "if I did not experience the frustration of not always being able to effect that crossing; if I never felt dissatisfied with one language, hearing in it the lack of the two others . . . my knowledge of these languages would be passive: mere information."[1]

---

1 Sylvia Molloy, "Presidential Address 2001: Crossings," *PMLA* (*Publications of the Modern Language Association*) 117(3) (2002): 407–13.

In *Varied Imagination* (2003) and *Living between Languages* (2016)—the two fiction pieces included in this volume—Molloy makes clear that living between places and languages highlights the performance of everyday life. Who and where we are shapes what we know and what we can recall. The short entries that make up each collection revolve around an interrelated set of questions. What makes "home"? Does language make or destabilize a sense of "home"? How does speaking a language, several languages, switching between languages perform one's place in the world? Language (dis)locates one as much as place does.

Sylvia Molloy's early home life was deeply shaken by language. Her Irish father and French mother were in fact both born in Argentina and conversed in Spanish. Legally, they were an "Argentine boy" and "Argentine girl," as she refers to them. Identity, however, had little to do with legal nationality. Identity was transmitted through language. Molloy's paternal family spoke British English. Molloy learned English from her father and grandmother, along with the customs and conventions that came along with it—such as high tea and a sense of social superiority. Molloy's mother, the youngest of eight children, never learned French from her immigrant family and was monolingual in Spanish. The Molloys and their acquaintances looked down on her. Young Sylvia felt "vergüenza" (shame) for her mother. She learned French for her; her multilingualism served as compensation for the presumed "poverty" inherent in monolingualism.

The domination of British English made itself felt in most aspects of daily life. Molloy shows how the monolingual bourgeoisie in Argentina used an English or French word as a "bilingual effect, not the work of switching but the work of citation." It's a performance, a way of showing (and showing off) that one belongs to a world wider and more sophisticated than the one ordinary Argentineans inhabit. Molloy's mother had perfected the British tea service as a way of impressing her husband's English visitors. "Morrti?" she would ask in a gesture of belonging. "Tankiou." This citational mix, re-enacted in each possible occasion, acknowledged England and France as enviable European centers of culture. Again, Molloy viscerally feels her mother's humiliation.

Multilingualism reveals a history of shifting locations and identities. Power dynamics, she notes, underwrite all bilingual acts, memories, and fantasies, but not in the same way. Molloy is acutely conscious of how the when/how/where of code-switching or *switcheo* or mixing enacts privilege and hierarchies across class, citizenship, and educational levels. In "Pérdida" [Loss], she uses multiple languages to perform how "[l]a mezcla, el ir y venir, el switching pertenece al dominio de lo unheimliche que es, precisamente, lo que sacude la fundación de la casa"—that is, "The mixing, the comings and goings, the switching, belong to the realm of the uncanny, which is precisely what shakes the foundations of the home." *Switcheo*, like language itself, is all about relationships not just to place, or to others, but to entire systems of power.

Our position within those systems changes according to the place(s) we occupy within them. Because *switcheo* is so profoundly disruptive of reigning colonial hierarchies dominated by British English, it needs to be stamped out. The "bilingual" school she attended was English-only in the mornings when minds were supposed to be alert. Violating this rule could lead to expulsion. No one seemed to care much what happened in the Spanish-language afternoons.

Acquiring a language is losing a language—Molloy acutely feels the "lack of the other" language as she converses in any one of them. There's always another word, another way of saying it. Her reflection on *switcheo* is tellingly called "Pérdida." Shifting places also feels like a loss. *Varied Imagination* opens with a loss of home. Literally. "Just before I leave for Buenos Aires, someone tells me that my parents' house is no longer there." The protagonist, who we assume to be Molloy, no longer lives in Argentina, and in fact stays in a hotel when she visits, but the thought that her family home has been torn down fills her with indignation. "How dare they [. . .]?" The title of that opening piece, "Casa tomada" [A House Taken Over], suggests a state of siege, past and present under erasure. The rumor turns out to be false, the home has been remodeled somewhat but remains recognizable and in place. But Molloy can return only through memories, hauntings, muddled recollections. *Varied Imagination* is a poignant drama of displacement, dislocation, and confrontation with a world and characters she thought she knew only to find nothing, and no one, was as she thought.

Her memories lead to her old home, the seaside, to World War II, to being molested by her family doctor as a child, to intuiting and owning her same-sex desires, to her ordeals with cancer. But everything looks different. She writes, "I recognized nothing." She's stumbling onto the wrong stage. She's looking for a past that she did not understand at the time, a past that doesn't exist, and maybe never existed. The siege or "assault" of memories "leave[s] a trace in your body, like a tremor." While she experiences the visceral blow, she can only intuit the cause. The tumultuous history of the 1940s and 50s of her childhood are known to her as silences, things unsaid, gestures. "I remember that on June 4th, 1943, my mother fetched me early from school [. . .] and kept looking up to the sky, as if searching for planes, as she hastily pushed me indoors. I thought that we were about to be bombed, like Europe. I then heard the name Perón for the first time."

Although Argentina was not bombed, the war in Europe played out everywhere in the country. Place, language, food—all participated in the Axis vs. Allies hostilities that split families and communities. Everything was murky. Were her cousins training to be Nazis? Was her mother's friend Jewish? Or a Nazi? Or both? Did her friend's husband know she was sleeping with someone else? No one seemed to "have a clue to what was going on." The indecipherability of the past, however, does not render one innocent. Her cousin, it turns out, was a Nazi, and a Peronist, according to her mother. He might also have been a torturer during Argentina's Dirty War (1976–83), Molloy hints, looking into her maternal family through online records. "I would not recognize him today." Yet, at her mother's funeral, he and Molloy co-signed the documents for cremation. Molloy tries to distance herself: "I felt contaminated, guilty," she tells someone. "I tried to set myself apart, I'm not in touch with him, I said; but I don't know if I was believed."

Memories of incidents undecipherable at the time come back to haunt Molloy's present:

> My grandmother died when I was four: I remember visiting her shortly before her death, I remember saying something to her, I don't know in what language. This not knowing what language I used needles me. In fact, I have used the episode on two occasions in fiction: In one version, the child speaks English and makes his grandmother happy before she dies; in the other, the child refuses.

Scenes of love, spite, and reconciliation are renegotiated in the present.

Memory can serve as an instrument of destruction, often through language. A spinster sister tells her younger widowed sister that her husband had a long sexual relationship with their gorgeous (now deceased) middle sister. Although the two sisters lived together, "they stopped speaking to each other. Not too much later they both died. [. . .] I would like to know what made the elder sister reveal her secret at the end of her life, when there was no possibility of settling accounts." Was it malice? And why, in another vignette, did an unnamed man, upon his death, leave his lover love letters from another woman (along with money in a safe)? Molloy taunts us: "I could have been the woman who found the letters; or the one who wrote them. I have changed a few details, invented others [. . .]" Is this Molloy's story? Or *a* story? Fiction and memory mesh and adjust to present exigencies. The past is not knowable—only fiction is. "Fiction always improves on reality."

Throughout these writings, Molloy recalls acts that seek to rewrite memory. Words spoken after a death that alter the meaning of a life, of a relationship. Triumphant dying words of glorious futures re-enacted daily for tourists for performative effect. Messages "that came to me forever late." What do we need to know to remember? *Varied Imagination* tells a version of Molloy's early life story that she cannot fully remember.

Living as a multilingual scholar in the United States, Molloy encountered another bilingualism, an "idioma intermedio" or "language in between." A Salvadorean construction worker speaks to her of "shirra" and "rufo" and "besmen" and "boila"—words that exist neither in Spanish nor English but necessary words meaning sheetrock, roof, basement, and boiler. "[W]e get along fine," both outsiders "[i]n a country that is not our own." But there are outsiders and outsiders, Molloy makes clear. After a pleasurable linguistic telephone "binge" with a friend in French, "with showy displays of adverbial clauses, lots of quand meme, tout compte fait, and par surcroit," she walks into the next room to encounter the Polish electrician who, excited by her "plurilingualism," points to the window and tries repeatedly to say something in English. *Birds*, it turns out, after multiple attempts at communication. "[A]nd I, full of myself and my self-conscious performance in French, had not even guessed at what he was saying. I felt very guilty."

These vignettes, whimsical, profound, painful, and witty, capture the realization that the most "natural" things in life—home, language, identity—depend largely on performance. Each communicates something, means something, does something to their audience. There is nothing settled about who we are or where we're from. Molloy always introduced herself as "from Argentina," but wherever she was, there was always an "elsewhere." And there is nothing "natural" about the languages we speak—language acts are situated. We constantly show others who we are, what we know, where we're "from" and where we've been, often, as Molloy makes clear, to show them up. For all her wanderings, Molloy admits at the end of *Varied Imagination* that a "sense of dislocation continues to haunt me." After 9/11, the balmy fall weather in the US transports her to spring in Buenos Aires:

I caught myself thinking a great deal about my mother, my father, my aunt, my sister: all dead. These were recollections or dreams (I can barely tell them apart) of a very distant past, when I still didn't know that I would not be spending the rest of my life in Buenos Aires. [. . .] I'm in Buenos Aires, I tell myself. I'm in my parents' house. No, I haven't left.

The first time that Sylvia Molloy and I spoke about rendering the brilliant *Vivir entre lenguas* in English was back in early 2017. It was January, and we were "sushiando," as we called our sushi lunches. I insisted that *Vivir entre lenguas* had to exist in English. Sylvia—she was always "my friend Sylvia" to me—had justified her decision to write this book about bilingualism in Spanish with the profound insight that "[q]uisiera o no, siempre se es bilingüe desde una lengua [. . .] aquella en que uno se reconoce" (Unavoidably, one must always be bilingual from one language [. . .] the language of fleeting self-recognition). Even though every person comes into being (or self-recognition) initially from one language, she goes on to clarify that it "does not mean [that's] the language in which one feels more at ease, or the language one speaks the best, much less the language one has chosen to write in." Yes, I argued, but this did not preclude, or exhaust, the rendering of bilingualism from the "other" language. Sylvia agreed. She had fragments written in English, and a few had already been published. She would rework the rest in English herself.

Years passed. Nothing happened. Neither of us remembered why. By January 2022, Sylvia was very ill with metastatic lung cancer. "Cancer doesn't forgive," she recalled her mother's saying. I would call her every week and hear her voice becoming weaker. "Me falta aire" (I need oxygen), she'd say. She expressed faith that the medications were working, that she'd make it back to Argentina in the spring, but she was clearly faltering. The desperation in her voice from her lack of air, breath, and by extension language, prompted me to suggest we get back to work on the book, *Living between Languages*. The transformation was remarkable. Her voice picked up. She got excited. And so we started again. Those last months, going back and forth through email, texts, and phone calls were a gift. For me, the gift was accompanying Sylvia. For her, she said it was a relief to talk about things other than shortness of breath, chemo brain, and edema.

The English version of the entries that make up this book started coming in as attachments—five and six at a time. At times Sylvia would lament she had mixed some up—the Spanish got tangled up with the English (totally in keeping with her thoughts about bilingualism). Some texts, we joked, resisted living in the other language. Computer problems added to the confusion. Soon Sylvia's life partner, Emily Geiger, was helping her cut and paste and sort and send the texts to me. Together we worked at a frantic pace. After she had finished, I worried she'd lose momentum. We decided that *Varied Imagination,* which she had also written though not published in English, was a necessary companion.

Even though Sylvia and I used the word "translation" in our emails and texts back and forth, neither of us thought of these new texts as translations but, rather, as crossings and re-articulations of texts from the earlier collection. As she puts it in "Titles" (recounting how she found an acceptable title in English for her novel, *El común olvido*), her process was "not a translation, not even a quotation, but the product of many goings back and forth between languages, which amounts to the same." In another piece, she writes, "I have dwelled on this shuttling between languages because it is the very stuff of my writing. It is often exhilarating, liberating; it is also laborious, fatiguing".

Both *Varied Imagination* and *Living between Languages* re-articulate many of the revelations that appear in the Spanish versions from this "other" language—the language that is not "el punto de apoyo" or "point of support." While following the logic and layout of the earlier books, Sylvia chose not to include versions of everything that appeared in the original. She omitted some texts, included new ones, and scrambled others. In *Varied Imagination* some pieces are rewritten to quite different effect. "Misiones," in Spanish, with its black snakes and menacing nature—a cross she says between Heidi and Conrad—is quite an agreeable place in the English: "a small inn in a little town in the jungle called el Hotel Suizo [Swiss Hotel]." It caters to international tourists "ready for [. . .]

typical food and adventures." In *Living between Languages* the "Afterthought" is now the "Foreword." Some texts remain the same but appear with different titles. Parts from "Punto de apoyo," for example, became "Punctum" and "Alteration." Some texts have the same name, "La lección de escritura" (Writing Lesson), but are entirely different. And the voice in this "other" language sounds different—the more one immerses oneself in it, the more striking the differences. Molloy changes gender, now fully owning the feminine "she". She seems less mischievous—there are fewer asides. Gone is the reference to monolingualism as "un mal incurable," and the English alphabet of her youth as "rigurosamente masculino." Although she recounts that she "could be funny in English in a way that I could not in Spanish," *Living between Languages* drops some of the funnier anecdotes. "Los chistes verdes se contaban en español," she recalls in "Territorio", and some last names are treacherous in translation, such as "*Kuntz*, pronunciado en inglés, suena igual que *cunts*. Es decir, vaginas; o mejor dicho, *conchas*."

We would be mistaken, I think, to imagine we're reading the same books in English. And this is not, as might be said of any translation, because each language contains its own nuances, inflections, or energy that might not find an equivalent in another. Here, Molloy is consciously using her "English" voice to address an English-language reader. It's a different relationship, and a different moment. Shifting her position, she knows, affects the task and performance of bilingualism: "how do you translate bilingualism, how do you convert the switching so that the effect of two languages working on each other, against each other, remains?"

While there is much I would like to add, I want to close by thanking Sylvia for entrusting me with this preface. When she asked me to write something short as the "editor" of this volume, I resisted. I wanted to write it as her friend and editor, but I promised to keep it very brief. She agreed. This volume, like *Varia imaginación* and *Vivir entre lenguas*, speaks for itself. It needs no preface or introduction. Rather, here I have shared how this book came to be. While we all agreed these texts needed to be in English, coming when it did offered Sylvia a way to breathe, to play with words, translations, "dichos." She wrote, rewrote, edited, and worked against all odds to find the right mix, "le mot juste," to express the "estar entre" that was her life. Language was more than a way to stay alive. Language was living. And here, Sylvia continues to live in, though, and between languages.

Varied Imagination

1.

FAMILY

A HOUSE TAKEN OVER

Just before I leave for Buenos Aires, someone tells me that my parents' house is no longer there. Actually the message is somewhat confusing, relayed by a third person. A friend who has just returned from Argentina says something to that effect to his wife, who gives me the news: Pablo went to Olivos and says that. It's not clear what it is that Pablo says, if the house has been torn down to make room for a new construction or if the house has been renovated to such an extent that it is no longer recognizable. Either of these possibilities is extreme, but of course, giving in to the dramatic urgency of the message, I choose the first one and react indignantly, how dare they tear down my parents' house?

Why is it that Pablo, who is much younger than I and probably had not yet been born or was very young when I left Argentina, cares so much about my parents' house? Because Pablo attended an English school next door and remembered how, during recess, boys invariably kicked balls into my parents' garden and had to go fetch them, apologizing to an old lady (my mother) who always came to the door in a foul mood. I must say that when Pablo and I discovered that we shared that memory, I felt as if I were discovering a lost relative. But I remember those encounters between my mother and the schoolboys with details that Pablo does not recall, or does not want to tell me he recalls. For example, that my mother, overwhelmed by the unending parade of boys coming for their footballs, had set in place a confiscation regime. Stray balls were only returned on Fridays, when school let out. As might be expected, this did not contribute to her popularity among the students who, during recess, seeing my mother through the fence walking in her garden, would shout out all sorts of vulgarities, with abundant reference to genitals, their own and otherwise. That was when my mother, who by that time was almost seventy, struck tragic poses against the privet hedge, first calling out to the teachers who, instead of keeping an eye on the students, were busy gossiping in a corner ("Teachers, say something to your students, they're being disrespectful"), then resorting to imprecations to no one in particular, of the type: "How could this dump call itself a school?" No, Pablo has never said anything about these tragicomic scenes, perhaps because he doesn't want to, or because during his time in school my mother had given up her confiscation practices; or perhaps because he just doesn't remember.

It bothers me that the news about the house should reach me just as I'm about to leave for Argentina, when I feel at my most fragile. Once settled in my hotel, I go out to lunch with friends; they ask me if I want to go for a ride and I say, trying to sound casual, why don't we go to Olivos? I find the house looking just the way it was the last time I saw it, a few years ago; not identical to the way it was when I lived in it (the new owners expanded the living room which now extends into the front garden) but it is still quite recognizable. Even the trees and bushes my mother liked, a bougainvillea out front, a weeping willow in the back, are still there. I calm down. Everything is in order.

When I get back I speak to Pablo, what possessed you to say that the house had been torn down?—it's still there. Pablo insists that it is completely changed, they've added what amounts to a new building to it, two stories, and also the patio out front is gone, and a huge tree I remember quite clearly. But the patio and the weeping willow were behind the house, not out front, I say, and the house has barely been added to, it remains the same. Pablo argues that no, it's no longer the same but another house, and that the tree was out front. I realize that it is useless to insist to the contrary. It's quite possible that both of us are right.

CURES

His last name was Quintana. I can no longer remember his first name but that was how my mother addressed him, hi there, Quintana (because Quintana was on friendly terms with everybody), you must come around tomorrow, the girls are sick. He was a registered nurse and paid house calls to give shots, I don't quite know what of, something that was supposed to cure flus and winter colds. The visit was as useless as it was festive since Quintana talked a blue streak and was funny, come on my dear, don't start crying because you'll really feel nothing, when Quintana gives a shot it cures on the spot, how can you think I'd hurt you, that's it, lie very quiet my dear, see you felt nothing and we're done, now for the next one, Quintana's leaving, folks, say goodbye to Quintana. He came and went like the wind, this Quintana. I just remember his voice, with its slightly provincial drawl, and the smell of his cologne. I remember too the small alcohol burner where he briefly boiled syringes and needles, and also the fact that my mother laid out a couple of perfectly ironed linen towels for him to wipe his hands after washing them and before applying the shot. Once in a while we would see his car parked in front of some house or we'd cross it on the avenue and my father would toot the horn and say, there goes Quintana, off to jab somebody's bum.

But above all I remember a day when I alone was sick and Quintana was called in. His wife had just died and he had lost his verve, he feels completely lost, my mother would say. This was obvious in his prattle, now forced, as if he were engaging in a performance that was no longer funny. He gave me the shot (it did not hurt) and told me he was very sad, and then he turned me over on the bed and pulled my knickers down around my thighs, let me look at you, sweetheart, and he patted me and said you look so like my wife, pobrecita, and for an instant he put down his head on my stomach and kissed me, and I saw his Brillantined hair real close. Then he got up and left.

I don't know where my mother was that afternoon, nor do I know if I told her anything. But she must have suspected something because Quintana never came back to the house. From then on we resorted to other cures for our colds and flus. They were just as inefficient.

ATLANTIC COAST

Two recollections merge in my mind. Vacations spent as a child in Punta Mogotes, in a very old hotel with a peeling facade. We drive past another hotel and my mother says casually that's where Edda Mussolini used to stay, Alberto says that one day he saw her, always alone. I vaguely know who Mussolini is, they tell me that Edda is his daughter, that she spent some time in Argentina. I imagine Edda Mussolini sitting on a rock and looking out to sea, her face very sad and a dark cape over her shoulders. This image clings to me. I ask my father repeatedly to drive past the hotel; I look carefully to see if I catch Edda Mussolini sitting on a rock. Later on I am told that a writer named Alfonsina Storni killed herself jumping into the ocean, from where, I demand to know. I imagine it may well be the rock where Edda Mussolini used to sit.

Punta Mogotes was sad but had no mystery. Mar del Sur, instead, was eerie, a sort of land's end, with only one hotel at the end of interminable dirt roads. I went there with my parents once, driving from Punta Mogotes, we wanted to have tea in the hotel which seemed to have no guests. We were alone in a dining room that I seem to remember was cold even though it was summer. A pianist played boleros, how badly this man plays, said my father who had not yet lost his hearing.

In 1987 I returned to Mar del Sur, out of curiosity. There was the hotel, as usual, now a shadow of what it had been. In the back, in what used to be the garden, there were remnants of demolition, bricks, pieces of concrete, strewn among the weeds. We had the feeling that someone was spying on us from a back window. When we went in through the front door, there were two people in the entry hall, who looked at us with vacant eyes and did not seem to understand our questions. We tried to go in further but were stopped by a woman with suspicious eyes and unquestionable authority who came to us saying that we could not go in. We objected; we would like to visit the hotel, inquire how reservations are made. She shot back: the hotel is not open to visitors and please leave immediately. This doesn't seem to be a hotel any longer, we told ourselves, there's an odd atmosphere. Could it be an asylum?

I also returned that time to Punta Mogotes, but everything looked so different that I recognized nothing. I did not find the hotel where Edda Mussolini used to stay. Someone said as a joke that it must be the Grand Sasso and I didn't understand the reference till it was explained to me.

SCHNITTLAUCH

Memories of the forties, of the beginning of the forties, assault me at times with the force of unresolved fears, those fears that leave a trace in your body, like a tremor. The usual uncertainties of childhood were compounded by others, hard to define. There was a war in Europe. I remember tag sales (after the war they would be called "American sales") held by Englishwomen to benefit the Allied forces, I remember that in one of those sales, my mother, who spoke no English and felt somewhat ill at ease in these events where the British community showed itself "at its brave and cheerful best," my mother, as I say, bought me a wooden horse, those that resemble a broomstick, with wheels at one end and a horse's head at the other. I remember hearing my mother say that my cousins, one of her sisters' sons who studied in the Military Academy, were only allowed to hear war reports favorable to the Axis. They're training them to be Nazis, she would say, with the relish of one predicting misfortune. I remember that on June 4th, 1943, my mother fetched me early from school, did not let me play outside in the garden, and kept looking up to the sky, as if searching for planes, as she hastily pushed me indoors. I thought that we were about to be bombed, like Europe. I then heard the name Perón for the first time.

My mother had a friend whose family was German. She believed this friend to be a Nazi although at the same time she would say that she was probably Jewish. The two of them had been schoolmates from first grade through high school. She suspected that Bertha came from a Jewish family but did not admit to it; and then she had married someone who came from a family of Nazi sympathizers but who did not admit to that either. The evidence on which my mother based her judgments was tenuous: on the one hand, there was Bertha's maiden name, that sometimes (but not always) was Jewish; on the other was the fact that in that house of music lovers, my mother claimed, no music by Jewish composers was ever played now, Mendelssohn was forbidden. I don't know how my mother knew this; her ignorance of music was faultless.

One summer, instead of vacationing on the beach as we used to, my mother, my sister, and I spent some time in Bertha's country house in Pilar. Was it to save money? Had my parents had a falling out? We slept together in one enormous room, my mother, my sister, and I. My father came to see us on some weekends, not all; we would go pick him up at the station in an old horse-drawn coach. Bertha had an old aunt living with her whom she called Tante Guitte, and my sister and I would call her, in fun, Tanta Guita, So-Much-Dough. She didn't like it one bit. I think I remember that my mother was sad.

I never understood the friendship between my mother and Bertha, of whom my mother would say that, besides being probably Jewish and a Nazi by marriage, she liked partying too much, and that the German (as everyone called Bertha's husband, including Bertha) didn't have a clue to what was going on. I now think that so much strangeness—the Jewishness, the Nazi sympathies, the cheating on the husband—constituted, for my mother, a dark zone, both attractive and repellent, in which that friendship flourished. Once in a while a friend of Bertha's would come spend the night; he was very nice and we called him Uncle Ernesto. He was also German, I don't know if Jewish, I don't know if Nazi. He slept with her.

I do remember the day they had an argument, my mother and Bertha, over something insignificant. My mother, who had volunteered to supervise the activities in the kitchen as a way, I think, of repaying Bertha's invitation, had herself prepared a rice dish which she garnished with chives. Bertha barely touched her plate. This mortified my mother, who, resorting to one of the few French words she remembered from childhood, perhaps because she felt insecure and wanted to magnify the importance of the rejected dish, asked: Don't you like ciboulette? What I don't like is Schnittlauch, this rice tastes like a cheap joint, Bertha answered, thinking she was funny. My mother got up and left the room.

On the following day they were friends again. My mother told me that she had had a bad night; I couldn't get to sleep, I remember her telling me, didn't you hear me? I spent hours saying "Schnittlauch" out loud until I fell asleep.

A MOTHER'S WISDOM

French occupies a complicated place in my life, one charged with passions. As a child I demanded to learn the language because it had been denied my mother. Born to French parents who stopped speaking French to their children after their third child, she didn't have a chance: she was number eight. Instead of speaking French to the family, my grandparents moved to Spanish, and spoke French only between themselves. I wanted to recover that mother tongue so that my mother, like my father, would have two languages. Monolingualism, I thought, was poverty.

French became even more inviting when I started studying French literature. I was dazzled by a teacher, barely ten years older than I. She was unhappy in her marriage, at least so they said. I adopted her literary preferences: Racine was better than Corneille, Proust more interesting than Gide. The latter choice was hard, just as it was hard later on, and also because of a woman, to go from preferring dogs to preferring cats—but love conquers all. The choice was hard because I secretly identified with Gide, with his Protestantism, with his endless moral debates over a sexuality that I divined to be my own even when I wasn't completely sure, with the effectiveness of some of his phrases, learned by heart and repeated like mantras, some of which I more or less remember: "Chacun doit suivre sa pente, pourvu que se soit en montant." Proust did not appeal to my ethical quandaries as an adolescent in the same way.

My French teacher wanted to practice her English and suggested that we exchange conversation lessons. I would go to her home two afternoons a week, when she was alone. Her sons, still quite young, were at school. We exchanged summaries of books we had read, we talked; she needed to perfect her spelling and asked for dictation. I remember once opening the book she was reading at random to dictate a paragraph, without paying much attention to content. I only recall that when I came to a sentence about the protagonist giving "a low, sexual laugh," or words to that effect, I was mortified, and struggled to keep going because I was afraid that she would realize something was going on, would think that I had chosen the passage on purpose. I always thought the book was H. D. Wells's *Tono-Bungay*, I don't know why. It was more likely D. H. Lawrence. I have tried locating the phrase ever since, without success.

The day came when my teacher told me she was leaving Argentina. Her husband, a French consulate officer, had been transferred to Istanbul. We had our last conversation class and then the husband came home and offered me a drink which went to my head. When it was time to say goodbye, I didn't know what to say and awkwardly shook hands, very formally, without saying a word. That night I slept badly; I wept. My mother noticed and I just told her I was upset because I hadn't bid Madame X a proper goodbye. The following day my mother handed me a couple of toys. These are for the children, she said; take them and tell her that you forgot to give them to her yesterday. That way you can give Madame X the kiss you didn't give her.

ILLNESS

The way in which one relates to illness is always complicated, driven by fear, negotiation, and superstition. When one is a child, responsibility for illness falls on the mother: in consultation with a thermometer, she's the one who decides when one is sick—the mother, not the body of the child. When one is a child, one doesn't know how to say "I am sick." When one is an adult, one doesn't know either: at least that is my case. I have had cancer twice. On both occasions, a tumor was excised. People would ask me, not too long after, how do you feel? and I would say "fine," but in truth I hadn't stopped feeling fine at any point, as if there was nothing wrong with my body—except for the fact that it had cancer. I feel fine; I have cancer. The present tense bothered me, I asked a consulting doctor how I should refer to illness, should I say "I have" or "I had." "I had," she said firmly. But then, three years later, "I had" another cancer.

I'm fully aware that I'm treading on dangerous territory. One doesn't fool around with illness, not even to relate its visitations. Maybe I should stop. But today I feel a pain on my right side and my body claims my attention. I feel ill today.

I remember a woman who lived one or two blocks away from the house where I grew up. We knew her because her daughters attended the same school as my sister and I, but contact with her didn't go beyond a cordial greeting or a conversation, now and then, between her and my mother. She was very beautiful. My mother admired the way she carried herself, so beautiful, so regal, she would say, so athletic. I thought I heard disapproval in the last adjective—not so in the other two. Through the window, as we were having lunch, we would see her go by, my mother and I. "There goes the Gómez woman," my mother would say, "so regal, just look at her, she has the world at her feet." I don't remember the way she carried herself as well as I remember her hips which were very narrow, like that of a young boy.

The Gómez woman, whose first name was Lucretia, a name the budding adolescent I had become found hugely suggestive, was diagnosed with breast cancer. In those days, the solution, if that's the correct term, was radical: she underwent a double mastectomy. She recovered quickly and we began to see her go by our house once again, always regal. "Look at the Gómez woman," my mother would say, "so beautiful again, so regal, so sure of herself. But," she would add solemnly, as if she had practiced the phrase many times, "cancer doesn't forgive." My mother—so adept at enumerating (and relishing) the misfortunes of others, endowing them with moral value.

More than once I thought back to that phrase when I had cancer and went daily to the hospital for treatment. I have repressed the radiation room, the nurses' faces, even the stretcher where, I know full well, I would lie down to receive treatment. In vain I try to conjure them up in my mind; I only get as far as the waiting room, then everything merges and becomes blurry. I do remember, however, the noise made by the radiation machine, something between a drone and a death rattle. That—and my mother's phrase.

COUSIN

I often resort to Internet browsers, not so much to look up something as to chance on interesting details, bits of gossip. As a child I would do the same with the telephone book. I would look up my father's last name to see who else, in Buenos Aires, carried it: a hopeless task, since the name, so common in Ireland, was unusual in Argentina. I also looked up my mother's maiden name, she did have relatives, and I would find her siblings, my aunts and uncles, and sometimes my cousins. I then looked up names of schoolmates, especially girls I wasn't friends with, girls whom I secretly envied, to find out what their parents' names were, and where they lived. I memorized the telephone numbers of some of my favorites; every now and then I would let drop the name of a street where one of them lived, say Juncal between Rodríguez Peña and Montevideo, and spied her reaction.

When I discovered the possibility of searching online, I recaptured that childish curiosity, the vicarious pleasure of spying on someone. I again looked up family names, this time less successfully, since few relatives remain on either side of my family and, I must admit, they are not famous. The telephone book was a democratic collection: all you needed to figure in it was a telephone, a luxury perhaps in

Argentina at the time, but one that a large number of people shared. The browser instead only gives names that are news, or literally in the news. Under my father's name I found some athletes, the name of a college in New York state, and I found myself. Under my mother's name I found French references. There were several entries devoted to functionaries, medical doctors, local glories of the South of France from where my grandparents had set forth to come to Argentina. I did find two Argentine references, one a woman who has distinguished herself in one of the sciences, I can't remember which, and who may well be a relative, the daughter of one of my cousins. The other entry is less innocuous. It appears in a list of names published by one of the groups of relatives of the "disappeared," a list that cites names of kidnappers, torturers, and other cohorts of the generals' terror regime. Going down the list I find my mother's maiden name and I recognize a cousin who occupied an important government post during the dictatorship.

I don't remember him all that well. I do remember how my mother despised him because he was, she said, a Peronist, and then she would correct herself and say no, he's a Nazi, and he's a Peronist because he was a Nazi before that, that's what he got out of the Military Academy. During the war, my mother would say, the cadets were only informed of Axis victories, never of Allied achievements. This cousin was quite a bit older than I was and I must have seen him three or four times in my life, at some birthday party, dressed up in uniform. I would not recognize him today.

One of the times I saw him was, coincidentally, my mother's funeral. After the ceremony I had to provide documents and authorize cremation. I signed, the signature of another relative was needed, and my cousin appeared, reminding me of who he was, and then, with the calm authority befitting a responsible relative, prepared himself to sign. I didn't dare refuse, even though I knew it was the last thing my mother would have wanted.

Time and time again I have gone back to that entry, as if wanting to wrench from it more information, some enlightenment. A short time ago, inexplicably, I found myself telling someone about my discovery. He looked at me with amazement and I felt contaminated, guilty. I tried to set myself apart, I'm not in touch with him, I said; but I don't know if I was believed.

2.

DYING WORDS

A few years ago, I visited Trotsky's house in Mexico City with my friend Miriam. We bought tickets, went out to the garden where the visit began, and were approached by a young woman who offered to be our guide. At first, we refused but she was so insistent that we finally gave in. She showed us room after room of that melancholy house, witness to a death that is reenacted daily. As the visit progressed, the young woman, with little or no subtlety, prepared us for the great event, building suspense, giving meaningful emphasis to her words, so that by the time we got to the study, she would have our undivided attention. Then the young woman really came into her own. She painstakingly explained where Trotsky was sitting, where Mercader, "the traitor of humanity," had been standing behind him, and how the deadly blow had been delivered. She told us that Trotsky had cried out; that Natalia Sedova, his wife, had rushed in from the next room to assist him; that Trotsky had managed to say to her, before being taken to the hospital where he died (and here the young woman deepened her voice): "This time they have succeeded, Natalia, but our cause, which is the cause of all humanity, will live forever," etc., etc. I loved this lengthy

oration at death's door, delivered with such emotion, for which Trotsky would have needed much more breath than was left in him after Mercader's precise blow. We gave the young woman a tip.

There's a rhetorical pleasure to perfecting what great men (never great women except Joan of Arc) may or may not have muttered when they found themselves in death's throes; an undeniable relish to be found in "Et tu, Brute"; "I die happy, we've defeated the enemy"; "Spain, I'm going to Spain"; "More light"; "Put down the light"; or "Rosebud." Later on I read somewhere that the last words Trotsky said to his wife, once in the hospital where they tried in vain to save him, were "Don't let them undress me, you do it." The pathetic intimacy of these words is more satisfactory. Yet nothing guarantees that they are any less apocryphal than the ones the young Mexican woman eloquently recites, every day, in her museum.

MISIONES

Several years ago, when traveling in the northern province
of Misiones in my native Argentina, a province adjoining
both Paraguay and Brazil, I stopped at a small inn in a little
town in the jungle called El Hotel Suizo. It was a small family
affair, run by descendants of German settlers (Germans
emigrated to that part of Argentina throughout the twen-
tieth century, for diverse reasons, too long to go into here).
"Swiss," even in these hinterlands, appeared to be a sign of
prestige and fine hostelry, a promise the Hotel Suizo did not
quite live up to. In spite of their clearly Nordic origins, the
owners spoke only Spanish and also some form of Guaraní
with their help. When my companion and I came down to
dinner, we found there were two other guests: A French couple, he excruciatingly morose, she friendly, even garrulous,
armed with a glossary and making very laudable efforts to
speak Spanish with the hosts. We wisely ordered something
simple, ignoring the wide array of appetizers basking in the
still-very-warm setting sun. The French woman was more
adventuresome, what do you recommend that is typical of
the region, she asked in reasonably good Spanish. I could
imagine the hotelkeeper's eyes lighting up as she answered
with perfect composure, "You must eat the berenjenas then."

On the appetizer table there was indeed a huge, largely untouched platter of stewed, pickled eggplant, a dish typical not so much of northern Argentina as of northern Italy. There followed a flurry of dictionaries and linguistic consultation, increased by the disruption of the Spanish/Arabic "jota," notoriously difficult for French lips. "Berenjena" was not in the book. "Aubergine," I pitched in, with some foreboding, having been raised by a mother with a commendable if exaggerated distrust for unrefrigerated foods. The couple accepted the suggestion with alacrity, marveled at the fact that "aubergine," a word of Arabic origin, was typical of the Argentine/Paraguayan/Brazilian region, and ate their way through heaps of the stuff. The following morning, with some guilt, I looked out for the couple, half fearful that they had succumbed to botulism. But no, there they were, cheerfully having breakfast and ready for more typical foods and adventures.

1914

The imaginary of war is mysterious, its inventions unforeseeable. World War I, nearly a century back, appears to be particularly rich in images and objects that allude to it, maybe because it's a war that, even today, keeps its aura of pathos: fields of France sown with white crosses, murderous trenches, very young soldiers with helmets or kepis, horses struggling in the mud, Fresnay who uses the formal address to speak to his mother and his wife, von Stroheim's geranium, *All Quiet on the Western Front*, the tango El Marne, an English unofficial rose. A world was coming to an end, or so they said.

As a child, when I visited my aunts, I liked to look at a print hanging on the wall of one of the bedrooms. It depicted a woman in a very large black lace headdress, a banner with an eagle at her feet, fainting into the arms of a brave solider who supports her with one arm and raises a French flag with the other. I would ask for its meaning time and time again: the woman was Alsace; the trodden banner, Germany; the soldier who saves her, France. This had happened in another war, not this one, they would tell me, a long, long time ago, before you were born. Besides the print, two other objects bore witness to this mythological war,

seemingly so different from the one I heard my parents worry about, which preceded my existence. One was at home and had belonged to my grandmother on my father's side; it was an ashtray consisting of a small brass bowl resting on a tripod made with three bullets. The other had belonged to my maternal grandmother; it was a crucifix made out of bullets, on a small pedestal, with a Christ made out, I was told, of molten bullets. The bullets that made up the crucifix were identical to the ones in the ashtray. From France and from England, relatives of one grandmother or the other had probably sent these mementos. The two families that had so little in common, despite my parents' marriage, were linked in Buenos Aires through these little tangible horrors.

I lost track of the print and the ashtray, not so the crucifix, which cropped up here and there during my life. When my aunt died, my mother brought it home for some reason and I caught sight of it now and then on her night table. Then, when my mother moved, my sister, who as a child shared my fascination for it, took it with her. A random remark to the effect that wars are always kitsch-producing engines because direct recollection would otherwise prove intolerable made me think of the crucifix once more, and I asked one of my nephews about its whereabouts. He handed it over to me when I next saw him; it was somewhat dented, but now it was mine. This time I looked at it closely, saw that there was writing etched on its base, and, with a magnifying glass, was able to decipher the word: Albert. As in Borges's story, the crucifix delivered a coded message, it pointed—not before the event but long after it—to one of the major disasters of that war. For a few days I wondered what I should do with this message that came to me forever late. Then I thought of it as a quaint literary detail and forgot about it altogether. Until today.

VICHY

I read Adam Nossiter's *The Algeria Hotel*. The title is taken
from the name of the hotel which, during Pétain's government, became the Ministry of Jewish Affairs in Vichy. Nossiter
recovers the abject past that the French, until recently, were
intent on silencing, he recovers it despite the resistance and,
in some cases, the lack of memory of the inhabitants of that
city. For the good families of Vichy, the Jews were not a problem, they did their thing, we did ours, although they were,
if truth be told, an élément étranger. At the same time (and
the paradox is only apparent), the same burghers told how
they (or a neighbor, or a cousin, or someone they knew) had
saved a Jew by hiding him in their home. The story of the
"saved Jew," a set piece, absolved them.

I remember my first and only visit to Vichy at the end of
the fifties to work on Valery Larbaud's archives. I remember
it was winter, and the famous Parc des Sources, with its
casino and the Orientalist folly of its thermal baths, sur-
rounded by faded pastel-colored mansions, seemed to be a
sad place, like a shabby French colonial city, or at least what
I imagined a shabby French colonial city might look like, say
Algiers, say Abidjan, say Saigon. Vichy had thought itself the
center of the world (the world that cured its ills with thermal

waters), the center of France (geographically and, in the forties, politically); it was now the mere capital of a province. So provincial was it that my arrival turned out to be an event. A timid, twenty-year-old foreign student was news for the local press. I was invited to lunch by the mayor and his wife, very impressed that someone from so far away ("lots of Argentines used to come to take the waters, you know, very rich Argentines") would come work on the obscure correspondence of an all-but-forgotten local son. In that house, for the first time, I ate an exotic vegetable (as befits a French colonial city) prepared in my honor: crosnes du Japon. I then visited Larbaud's widow who had completely lost her Italian accent and who, I was told by my guide the librarian, was made to dress like a little girl by her husband, c'était pour le moins curieux, n'est-ce pas.

I was twenty, I didn't think of the past, I didn't put things together. I was amused, yes, that the sedate author of *Fermina Márquez* indulged in pedophilic fantasies. Only now, forty years later, on reading *The Algeria Hotel*, do I realize that the good burghers who offered me their hospitality had surely spent the war in Vichy, that they had probably seen the Maréchal when he strolled through the Parc des Sources or when he came out on his balcony, every Sunday, to greet the students who came to (quite literally) sing his praises; that they had seen other things, perhaps. (I believe the librarian who escorted me everywhere was called Madame Vignac. Nossiter interviews someone by the same name, maybe her, with little success: she remembers nothing.) But none of this came up during that luncheon, and I did not ask. For many years all I remembered from Vichy, besides its architecture, which, very soon, merged with so many others, was the old and frail Madame Larbaud, whom I mentally dressed up as a little girl, and the elusive taste of the crosnes du Japon, that I have not tasted since.

PATAGONIA

I'm interested of late in accounts of travel through Patagonia, fully aware that I'm giving into a fad. But beyond a vaguely cultural curiosity, Patagonia is for me the stuff of childhood memories, one in particular. My father, the director of a meat-packing business, traveled once in a while to Río Gallegos. Maybe this is his first trip I'm remembering; otherwise I can't understand all the ceremony. A company car comes for him at dawn and my mother, my sister, and I go with my father to the airport to bid him goodbye. At the time (it must have been the mid-forties) the domestic airport was little more than a few ramshackle sheds, and at dawn (or it might have been later, in winter it's still dark at six) they were practically empty. A tired-looking waiter, behind the counter, prepares coffee. He has the radio on, I hear a tune that for years I will remember as the saddest music I know. I must have been eight. We have breakfast, we say goodbye to my father, my mother weeps a little (this would seem to confirm that it was his first trip) and says to him, Come back soon, viejo. The company car takes us back home. Day begins to break. I also think it's raining, but I may be remembering a film I need not name.

This unusual recollection (why did the plane leave at dawn, why did we all go to the airport to say goodbye?) is completed by another which also signifies, for me, Patagonia. On his return from one of his trips, perhaps that first one, my father tells me that Patagonia is swept by harsh winds, winds so strong, he tells me, that they often knock down sheep, and the sheep, because of all their wool, cannot right themselves up and just lie there, on their side, until they die. Sometimes, before they're quite dead, buzzards come and peck their eyes out. Until this day I cannot understand why my father told me this story, knowing how much I loved animals, knowing how much it would distress me.

Years later, as an adolescent, I again heard the sad tune playing at the airport at dawn and asked what it was. "Heart-ache," I was told.

VARIED IMAGINATION

After my father died, my mother withdrew more and more into a world of her own, made up of memories and, above all, speculations of an invariably catastrophic nature. She knew little of my life, only the miserly portion that I uncharitably gave her to ward off her questions. What I didn't tell her, she filled in with her imagination. And she worried. She worried about money, or rather my lackadaisical relation to money, so different from hers; she worried about my friends. The phone would ring and she would answer, it's for you, she'd say. Is it a man or a woman, I'd ask, trying to place the caller. I don't know, she would answer in an exasperated tone, what strange friends you have, my dear. One day she said all of a sudden, I'm worried about something and we must talk, tell me something, do you have a child in Paris? The question took me by surprise and at the same time relieved me; I burst out laughing. You go there so often I don't know what to think, she said, somewhat offended, and I regretted having laughed. But you do have somebody there, she insisted. I said I did and, in turn, invented a lover, yes, and what's his name, Julian. What a strange name for a Frenchman, she remarked. Not so, there's a church in Paris, and also a writer, and also a wine, Juliénas. I said all this to allay her suspicions, to avoid telling her that yes, it was an unusual name; that, in addition, it was the name Vita Sackville-West took on during her escapades to Paris with Violet Trefusis. So literary of me—I had just read those letters.

My mother asked me once in a while about this imaginary lover. I think she recognized the fabrication yet needed to believe it. Two or three years later, during another visit to Buenos Aires, I decided to put an end to the charade and told her that Julian was, in reality, a woman. She demanded to know her name, and when I told her, she shot back, she's Jewish, and would not believe me when I said no. Then she wanted to know if this person had ever been married, I don't quite know why. Divorced, I said, and then my mother replied that she imagined the woman a blonde. Out of a bottle, she added, after a pause.

Later in the day my mother said she wanted to go out for a walk and asked me to come with her. She was quite frail and needed to lean on someone. We walked across the square in Olivos, parched and dusty, and she said she wanted to go in the church. My mother was not particularly religious. She sat in a pew, she may have prayed, while I walked down the aisles, looking distractedly at that church devoid of all charm. We did that, my mother and I. When we left the church she said: I don't know much about that kind of love. I suggested we have lunch out and she agreed. She ate with inordinate appetite.

It wasn't true that she didn't know, of course. Twenty years earlier, when the *Charles Tellier* was about to sail for Le Havre taking me to study in France and the bell rang to warn visitors that they should go on shore, she took me aside and said: In Europe there are older women who look for young secretaries, but it isn't secretaries they want. Without another word she kissed me goodbye, leaving me bewildered. I reminded her of the incident while we were having lunch. Really, she said, surprised; I don't remember a thing.

3.

CITATIONS

CEREMONIES OF EMPIRE

My mother, who did not come from an English family, had adopted the cult of tea-making with a convert's zeal. In tea-rooms, when she ordered, she would always specify "with cold milk" and would invariably add: "You always must tell them because they never know." Or else, when the silver-plated teapot arrived, piping hot, and she took her first sip, she would call the waiter back: "Waiter, this water never boiled." I remember that on one occasion an offended waiter shot back at her that the water had been boiling since morning. "See?" my mother said to me triumphantly, and then, to the waiter: "Tell them in the kitchen that water must be poured on tea as soon as it begins to boil. If it has overboiled it's as bad as if it had never boiled at all." I made an effort to look in another direction in order to avoid the waiter's face.

On weekends, at home, my sister and I were assigned the task of preparing tea. We knew full well that we couldn't skip a single step of the process, from warming up the teapot and precisely measuring the required amount of Misiones tea (that might not be English but was certainly as good) to pouring in the freshly boiled water, because my mother would discover our carelessness on her first sip.

Acquaintances of my father's often came to tea then, Englishmen who were traveling on business accompanied by wives who couldn't speak a word of Spanish. As soon as they came into the house, the husbands gathered around my father to talk shop; my mother had to entertain the wives; I was the go-between. The wives, whom my mother, in a more secure setting, might have described as drab, were generally pleasant, distant, and admiring of my fluency in English. They also, without exception, praised my mother's tea. Seizing on the chance to utter the few words she knew in English, my mother would say "Tankiou." Or else, when offering them another cup, "Morrti?"

When they got up to leave, I had to translate for my mother that they had had a very good time, and "tell your mother her tea was delicious." My mother would instruct me, in turn, to ask them if they wished to wash their hands. As a rule, they didn't understand the euphemism. On one occasion, one of these wives laughed heartily at my suggestion and said that she didn't, but did I think she should? Her husband joined in the laughter, so did my father. I never asked that question again.

GRAMMAR

As a child I demanded to learn French, the language of my mother's family, even though my mother didn't speak it. Her parents had abandoned it little by little as the family grew. They had spoken it with the older children; then they only spoke it between themselves. One could say that my mother was born monolingual.

I began speaking French cautiously, afraid to make mistakes. I learned grammar rules by heart and recited French verbs before I fell asleep. My French would be a native language, as if there had been no interruption between my grandparents and me; it would be as native as my English, which had not skipped a generation. (Spanish did not appear to have a genealogy: it simply was.) I gave French names to some of my dolls, the ones I thought prettiest. The French teacher who came home congratulated me on my pronunciation.

Two of my mother's sisters would sometimes come to visit, the firstborn, who had spoken French with her parents as a child, and a younger sister who, like my mother, did not speak it. One day I told them I knew how to speak French and the oldest aunt, perhaps happy to renew contact with the past, asked, as if to test me, "Qu'est-ce que tu vas faire demain?" Sure of my new knowledge and limited in my command of French verbal forms, I told her that she didn't know how to speak, that she should have said, "Qu'est-ce que tu feras." My aunt insisted she had expressed herself correctly; my mother and other aunt, who couldn't speak French and were perhaps resentful of this older sister who had learned the language from their parents, declared me correct. There was an argument; my older aunt wept, my mother and my other aunt, as if they were carrying out some secret revenge, were adamant: what Maria spoke was pidgin French.

One month later, in class, I learned other possibilities for the future tense in French. I realized my aunt Maria had been right; but I never told her.

THE USES OF LITERATURE

At school I learned poems in English, Spanish, and French by heart. I remember little of the Spanish ones, although a few useless lines linger in my memory: "Amé, fui amado, él solo acarició faz," and one or another verse by Bécquer. In English, I remember bits of Shakespeare, only bits though, since in class we never got to recite a text in its entirety. The majestic, unforgettable Englishwoman who had us read most of the plays, from age nine through age sixteen, measured our learning in a strange way. Let's say she had assigned Shylock's speech to Antonio in *The Merchant of Venice*. She would stride into class, open the register, ask us to shut our books, and then, quite arbitrarily, point to a student with an imperious, claw-like finger: "You," she would say, and the student would begin to recite "Signor Antonio many a time and oft," but the finger would stop her and move on to another student, "Now you!" and that student would continue, "In the Rialto you have rated me," but the finger was already pointing to yet another student, "About my monies and my usances," and so it went, at random, without following any foreseeable order except the one imposed by the capricious finger. The trick was not to let one's mind wander, to be always on the alert, so that the English finger would not catch us unprepared and we could get the following line right. In spite of this haphazard method, I remember a good part of Shylock's speech, perhaps because it relates to injustice, something that, as an adolescent, I was particularly sensitive to; or perhaps because the expression "Jewish gabardine" amused us; or perhaps I remember the speech because I was afraid, as we all were, of the imperious Englishwoman. In those classes, literature was reduced to a mere game of chance. It wouldn't have surprised us if the Englishwoman, when someone made a mistake, would have shouted out, like the Red Queen, "Off with her head."

I discovered other advantages to literature later on, this time in French. Racine's texts, also learned by heart, served to channel my unrequited love as an adolescent and to console me from deception as an adult. When I discovered I was embroiled in a love triangle I had not suspected, Phaedra's jealousy became mine and her "Comment se sont-ils vus" acquired the value of a mantra. And Berenice's adieus, recited to myself as I disconsolately walked the streets of Buenos Aires, made a definitive separation more bearable. But that is, as they say, another story.

CLOSING UP A HOUSE

When my father died, my mother decided that the house where they had lived for so many years had gotten too big for her (that's what she said, as if she were speaking of a piece of clothing) and sold it nearly immediately. She was given two months to empty it out, during which she proceeded to buy a small apartment a few blocks away, in the same neighborhood so that I don't feel homesick, she said. She also asked for our help in the move; without planning it, my sister and I arrived in Buenos Aires the very same day and started sorting things out and labeling them. We put things in five piles that corresponded to five clear-cut categories, or so we thought: things that were going to the new apartment; things that were going to be sold; things my mother did not want but my sister or I did (the latter category was subject to some dispute); things that were going to the Salvation Army; things that were going into the garbage. Everything went relatively well until my mother decided to review the piles and question our criteria for selection. She would take an object from one pile and put it in another, I may need this, but no, you agreed this went to the sale, your pile is the one over there, no, not that one, that goes out in the garbage, but how are you going to put that in the garbage if it's something your father gave you, OK, who is the one deciding here, you girls or me? When we finished, it was quite late and the three of us were barely speaking to each other. It is quite possible that my mother, who had trouble sleeping, continued moving things from one pile to another during the night.

Years later one of my friends had to empty out his mother's house after she died. His sisters decided to give away her clothes to charity without going through them, just like that. They even gave away her wedding dress, my friend said, when I looked out the window, I saw how they were loading that specific bag onto the truck. Who would find use for that dress, he said, not without reason. His story struck me as improbable but nevertheless effective. People like to fabricate farewell scenes, especially if they're pathetic.

And by the way: when she left the house to go to her new apartment, my mother, with a perfectly blank expression, ran her fingers along a doorframe, pressed the palm of one hand against a wall, let her fingers rest briefly on a doorknob. She was saying goodbye. It took me a while to realize that she was repeating a scene from a Garbo film. Without probably realizing it, my mother was quoting. This fact does not diminish the sincerity of her gesture; rather, it confirms it.

4.

DISTRUPTION

SISTERLY LOVE

They were three sisters, very close to each other, first generation Argentines, born to Spanish immigrants who raised them with an iron fist, intent on fostering their virtues, marrying them off well, and having them come up in the world. The parents achieve their goal. The youngest marries a lawyer, I don't think she was the best looking; at least that's what they say. That distinction goes to the middle sister, extravagant, she belongs in a music hall, said the less charitable relatives. This one, late in life (late in life, at the time, meant you were over forty), marries a widowed doctor with two children. The eldest daughter does not marry, continues to live with her parents, taking care of them till the end. As this is a long-lived family, she is set free (if that's the word) at sixty. Free and exhausted, I remember that as a child I was struck by the many wrinkles on her face and by her smile, like a grimace; but I did like her eyes, heavy-lidded and blue. When the showy one appeared, however, all eyes went to her. She often wore a turban and struck poses, as if she were about to be filmed, I'm ready for my close-up, Mr. De Mille.

She was the first to die, of the same ailment Eva Perón had died of, an ailment which at home was only referred to euphemistically. "They emptied her out," they would say of Evita, as if it were an unavoidable retribution, probably deserved. The younger sister then lost her husband and, since the sisters had been so close, she set up house with the remaining sister, the eldest, who never married. They sold the old family house because it made them too sad, and together they bought an apartment. With much enthusiasm, I seem to recall, in spite of their advanced age, they started out anew. A few years passed and I asked after them, curious to know how they were getting along. Not so well, I was told, they barely speak to each other after what happened. It seems that not too long after they started living together, the eldest sister told the youngest that her dead husband had had an affair with their extravagant sister, that for years, even after she married the widower with two children, they had seen each other, in hotels, in cars, sometimes in the bathroom of her very own house, during some birthday party; they couldn't stop seeing each other. The youngest sister wept, cursed her sister for telling her what she couldn't bring herself to believe, and then went on weeping when the other one showed her letters from the dead sister which took her, the eldest, as confident and accomplice, invoking sisterly loyalty and swearing her to silence. After that they stopped speaking to each other. Not too much later they both died, two months apart from one another, not from any unmentionable ailment but simply of old age.

I would like to know what made the eldest sister reveal her secret at the end of her life, when there was no possibility of settling accounts. Was it precisely for that reason? Or was it to experiment a power that had been denied her all her life, she, the sacrificial spinster who never complained and took care of their parents? But what surprises me even more in this passionate tale is the fact that the reprobate husband was well known to me, he was my mother's youngest brother, a gruff, sometimes harsh uncle I didn't much like. I have trouble imagining him as the protagonist of this uncontrollable passion, which should make me revise the picture I have of him. I'm unable to do so: like his wife, I come too late.

MISERY'S CHILD

When my father died, abruptly, in an automobile accident abroad, my mother, who was with him and survived, felt completely dislocated. I traveled to join her and accompanied her back to Buenos Aires. She withdrew into herself, started to behave strangely. She would look up at the moon and say, "Your father is up there." She seldom said anything, and when she did, she spoke, above all, of her childhood. She would say that as a child she had gone hungry, there were so many of us and mother had to work miracles. That was the first time I had heard her tell this woeful tale of indigence, and I was surprised. But you weren't poor, I countered, for lack of something to say. She didn't reply but the following day, at dinner time, she told me the same story while she end-lessly folded and unfolded her napkin, oblivious to the food before her. "Why don't you eat?" I said, as one coaxing a child, and she obediently complied, awkwardly moving her fork around in her left hand since her right arm was in a cast. This scene repeated itself several nights running, the story of the hunger suffered in childhood unvarying, her lack of appetite always the same. I realized that she had projected one deprivation onto another. I'm hungry, she was telling me, and there is no food to appease my hunger.

CONTEMPTIBLE

A man dies. In the safe, together with some money he leaves his lover, the mother of his son, are all the letters sent to him by another woman with whom he had a relationship at the same time. Of course it's the lover who opens the safe. He had said so many times: All that is in there is yours.

After the foreseeable reactions (anger, loathing, but above all terrible grief, less over him than out of a sense of total waste), the woman asks herself what to do with the letters. She could return them to the sender but that would be telling her that she's aware of the role the other woman played in the life of the man she loved; she rejects that course of action that in some way puts her in a weak position. Nor does she dare throw them out, because they're letters written by him, and because one doesn't throw letters away, even when they're addressed to someone else, she did this with letters from her mother to her father and now regrets it. Besides, she thinks, some day, when it no longer matters to her, she will read the letters from beginning to end (why not?), and it will not be intolerable. After all, everything that's there belongs to her, he himself said so. So she locks the safe after taking the money. And she also locks the apartment, leaving her vague plans for the letters for a future that never takes place, since she moves with her son to France. Fearing bad luck, she neither rents nor sells the apartment. Someday I may have to come back to Argentina and I want a roof over my head.

Years later, after his mother's death, the son returns to Argentina. He's practically a tourist: he speaks Spanish haltingly and feels more at home in French. He wants to empty out the apartment that belonged to his father, about whom his mother spoke so seldom and then with bitterness. It's as if he were traveling back in time. The apartment is in the same state it was ten years ago, the bed (I remember that bed) unmade since then, the towels hanging on hooks in the bathroom, the dishtowels in the kitchen, rumpled as if they had just been used to wipe the dishes. He finds a couple of photographs of a man who may or may not be his father. He tries to detect a likeness with himself but fails. He calls in a locksmith to open the safe and finds the letters. He realizes by the tone that they're love letters, some obscene, some sentimental, the woman who writes them addresses the man with a private name, like a secret between them, and she herself signs with a nickname. The son does not understand most of the allusions in the letters but concludes (although at the beginning he doesn't recognize the handwriting) that these are letters from his mother to his father. He also concludes that they loved each other passionately and this relieves him, enabling him to build an image of his father. He sells the apartment and returns with the letters to France.

I could have been the woman who found the letters; or the one who wrote them. I have changed a few details, invented others; I have added a character. Fiction always improves on reality.

CLAIR DE LUNE

My sister died on a New Year's Day, one of her sons found her the next morning lying next to her bed, dead of a hemorrhage, already stiff. The activity that ensued was feverish, as if my nephews and I had wanted to settle everything very quickly, put order in what had been an aimless life. I traveled to give them a hand, we took care of the funeral, of the paperwork, we finished everything in three days and then a terrible snow storm began, I was able to take the last plane out just before they closed the airport, as I had done so many times in Buenos Aires just before a state of siege. I returned home relieved, as one who has narrowly missed a calamity, feeling empty.

Two days later I went to the Caribbean to rest, to not think about my sister. It was an odd week, like a living contradiction, the sky so dazzlingly blue, the sea so transparent one could see now and then a giant sting ray at the bottom, lying in wait. The island was barely inhabited and relied on a more important island nearby for supplies, its economy depending exclusively on a cheap, makeshift kind of tourism. We rented a small apartment that gave onto the beach, backed by an empty, fenced-in area, the use of which was unclear.

I slept a great deal during those days. One night, however, I couldn't close my eyes. I thought of my sister, I couldn't get out of my mind an incident that had taken place just after the funeral. My nephew and I had left the house for a moment and when we came back, his wife, looking alarmed, drew me aside. I saw your sister on television, she said, and I thought she was raving. She explained that some channel had devoted a segment of the news to the increase in sales during the holiday season and my sister had suddenly appeared on the screen, tottering, with a gallon of Scotch under her arm, queuing up to pay in a liquor store. She had dark shades on but there was no doubt it was my sister; she had been filmed the day before her death. I don't want him to see the evening news, my nephew's wife said, they may repeat the same segment and I don't want him to see her, he was the one who found her dead. For my part, I would have given anything to see the news; I didn't have a recent image of my sister alive.

Moonlight filled the room, and as I couldn't sleep, I went out on the back balcony. I barely had to adjust my eyes since the full moon made it easy to see. In the empty lot behind the apartment, white with light, four or five cows were jumping about and playfully butting into each other, excited by the moon. They mooed with delight, seemed extremely happy, and I felt strangely comforted. I had never seen cows dancing in the moonlight. But then I had never seen a dead woman on the television screen the day of her funeral. I am haunted by those two very distinct images: one perceived, the other imagined, both unforgettable, forever joined in my mind.

ATMOSPHERICS

In September 2001 the atmosphere changed, my atmosphere. I don't mean that the events of the 11th made me feel fragile, uncertain about the future, although I certainly had those feelings. I mean the temperature, the seasons felt different, as if the attack on the World Trade Center had disarranged something within me in a much deeper way. In New York the day of the attack was magnificent; it felt more like spring than fall, with very clear skies and a glorious sun. As many clocks near the catastrophe stopped, so did the weather, suspended during weeks, months, in that mild sunny day. We waited for winter but winter never came. Plants started to sprout as if spring were about to begin, skies continued to be blue, it hardly rained. That was when I started to dream of Buenos Aires night after night. That was when I caught myself thinking a great deal about my mother, my father, my aunt, my sister: all dead. These were recollections or dreams (I can barely tell them apart) of a very distant past, when I still didn't know that I would not be spending the rest of my life in Buenos Aires; memories of childhood and adolescence. I dreamed of (or remembered) tones of voice, expressions buried deep in my memory, disjointed images, usually of happy times; all this despite the roar of helicopters over New York—although that also brought back a different Buenos Aires I still fear to recall. I believe the weather, that radiant never-changing fall, contributed a great deal to my sense of displacement, that weather I persisted in thinking belonged in Buenos Aires: since it was warm in October, it would be even warmer in November, classes would then be over, and Christmas would smell of freesias and gardenias.

This sense of dislocation continues to haunt me, prevents me from settling into a familiar chronology, much less into the reverse seasons I had such a hard time getting used to when I first changed hemispheres. I am writing this in April but for moments I think it is September. I know we're about to enter summer but there are days when something tells me that winter is about to arrive, with its rains and its clamminess; I even seem to feel it in the cool breeze that sometimes picks up in the evening. And I also feel it in the desolate barking of a dog, in the building opposite ours in New York, the same dog that used to bark in the house next door in Olivos when it started getting cold in the evening. I'm in Buenos Aires, I tell myself. I'm in my parents' house. No, I haven't left. It's getting cold, I should be going in.

Living between Languages

AFTERTHOUGHT AS FOREWORD

When I write, I still have trouble with beginnings, feel at a loss when starting a new piece. I have learned to trick myself into writing by resorting to the other language, whichever language the piece will not be written in. So I start out in that language, which I find easier because it is temporary, irrelevant, in a sense wasteful: it will not last. The ploy, for all its laborious artifice, usually works. After a while, I stop and translate myself into the language the piece will be written in, less threatening now that it has been exposed to the other language preparing its way. The practice of translation, forced as it is in this case, eases my entrance into the writing I initially feared. As I see it, it is an exercise in contamination; a most salutary one.

CHILDHOOD

To simplify matters I sometimes say I'm trilingual, that I was brought up trilingual, although come to think of it, the statement misleads more than it explains. Besides, it's not entirely accurate: I did not learn the three languages simultaneously but in succession, each language occupying a space and taking on an effect of its own. I spoke Spanish (or Castellano, as it is called in non-Castilian Argentina) first. Then, when I was three and a half, my father started speaking to me in English. Also when I was three and a half, my sister was born; instead of throwing dishes out the window, like Goethe when faced with a sibling, I acquired another language, which is another way, I guess, of breaking with safety. French was to come later; it did not coincide with any birth; it was more like a repossession.

FAMILY ROMANCE

Like many English immigrants of her generation, my grandmother, my father's mother, spoke bad Spanish. She had trouble remembering the word for "teapot" and, much to her son's glee, would ask not for a "tetera" but a "tetada," a titty, of tea. It upset her that I didn't speak English very early on, that Spanish was my first language. I think it also upset her that my father had married an "Argentine girl." It never occurred to her that my father was himself an "Argentine boy"; she just did not think of him that way. Immigrants and their offspring, regardless of their place of birth, were thought of in terms of language; they were their language. My mother had lost the French of her childhood; she was monolingual, left out in the cold, therefore Argentine. My father spoke English with his mother and sisters, Spanish with his wife and friends. Sometimes people called him "Che, inglés." My grandmother died when I was four: I remember visiting her shortly before her death, I remember saying something to her, I don't know in what language. This not knowing what language I used needles me. In fact, I have used the episode on two occasions in fiction: In one version, the child speaks English and makes his grandmother happy before she dies; in the other, the child refuses.

LANGUAGE LESSONS

The fact that my mother does not speak English makes Spanish mandatory in all gatherings with my father's family. My aunts, who are perfectly bilingual, condescendingly adapt. I feel ashamed. When they speak to me, I answer in English to show off, to make them see that I am not monolingual like my mother. "Talk in Spanish so Margot understands," they tell me. I seethe.

I remember that when I was still a child, my mother took English lessons from an English neighbor, a woman whose name I have forgotten although I do remember perfectly where she lived: next to the hospital. I remember the small yellow notebook in which my mother wrote down everything she learned. I remember how angry she got when she caught me one day going through that notebook she so carefully kept in her handbag, full of language exercises that were not too different from the ones I was given to do at school.

I don't know when she stopped taking those classes. I do know the notebook disappeared and my mother continued to be monolingual. The bilingualism that could have been hers, the one her French parents deprived her of, remained, as a leftover of sorts, in some conversations overheard at home. She and her sisters, when speaking of fashion or of needlework, still used French words, words that I remember even today, although I don't always know what they mean. For example, the word "soutache." Like small islands of the other tongue, they floated in the conversation. Maybe they brought back precise recollections of their semi-bilingual childhood; or maybe they were one more affectation of the Argentine middle class. In any case they allowed me to construct a less forlorn image of my mother.

LOSS

To "lose" a language. "A mind is a terrible thing to lose," said Dan Quayle, famously misquoting the motto of the United Negro College Fund. A language is also a terrible thing to lose. There were eleven siblings in my mother's family. The three oldest spoke French as children with their parents, a thick, southern French, I imagine, and then the family became monolingual. Did the parents, my grandparents, continue to speak this French in private when they confided in each other, when they made love? No one can answer my question. It's as if French in that family were in the closet. I think: Had I had children, in what language would I have spoken to them? Which language would I have repressed?

Because French was my mother's language, I decided early on to recover it for her sake. I didn't want my father to be bilingual and not my mother. I was quite young when I demanded to learn the language and a teacher was hired, an old friend of one of my mother's aunts, to give my sister and me French lessons. We called her Madame Suzanne. At the beginning she would throw up her arms in despair when we, not knowing a word in French, resolutely Frenchified its Spanish equivalent. Le café, we ventured, was stirred with une cucharite. In the meantime, Madame Suzanne herself, in speaking to our mother, did the same thing in the opposite direction: she would give my mother a recipe for crème anglaise and tell her she had to "hacer atención que no se atache," by which she meant she must see that it not stick to the pot. These examples refer (or attach themselves, like the crème anglaise) to home, to the spoon, the pot: they create a heimlich effect, even if the languages of the bilingual subject are rarely that. The mixing, the comings and goings, the switching, belong to the realm of the uncanny, which is precisely what shakes the foundations of the home.

J'ECRIS MA LECTURE

I spoke Spanish first but I read first in English. I was taught the alphabet phonetically by a Mrs. Richardson who barely spoke Spanish. Once I learned to read in English, I merely transposed the sounds to Spanish and read in that language too. One day my aunt found me reading out loud. "I can't believe it, she's learned to read all by herself!" she excitedly told everybody. I basked in my precociousness and did not have the heart to disabuse her. I was merely translating sounds.

Even as a child I knew I wanted to write, but I did not know how to begin. I would read instead, voraciously, everything that came my way, and then mainly in English. The only books I read in Spanish were the books my mother kept on her night-table and read before turning off the light, books I sneaked in to read, unnoticed. They were all translations from English: Margaret Mitchell, Pearl Buck, Louis Bromfield, later on Curzio Malaparte and Alberto Moravia, until my mother discovered my clandestine reading and hid her "adult" books. I went back to Nancy Drew.

As far as I can remember, I read only one French book in Spanish translation, *Memorias de un asno*, by the Comtesse de Ségur. I read it when I was quite young and, needless to say, identified with Cadichon the donkey and wept at his misery. The book's cruelty and pathos marked me for life. Madame de Ségur's emotional manipulation and perverse thrills are hard to revisit, however. Not too long ago, I purchased an old copy of the original in the Bibliothèque rose illustrée edition, wanting to know "how it sounded" in French. I have never brought myself to open it.

TERRITORY

Each language has its territory, its appropriate time, its rank. The school I went to as a child was divided in two: English in the morning, Spanish in the afternoon. It was, therefore, a bilingual school, but everybody thought of it as an English institution, un colegio inglés. This was due no doubt to the prestige attached to the term, but no less to the rules of the school. If a student was caught speaking Spanish in the morning, she was punished. She had to go to the principal's office, where she signed a black book, which turned out to be a tatty little black notebook, less ominous than it sounded. If you signed three times, however, you were expelled. Other serious offenses that led to signing the black book and to eventual banishment: wearing your socks rolled down, having your hair untied, or cheating on a test. These were serious offenses (as arbitrary as mortal sins in the Catholic church) but to speak Spanish during the English morning period may well have been the worst. In the afternoon, classes were taught in Spanish. If someone spoke English, no one cared; there was no punishment. Compared with English, Spanish was a lackluster language, at least for those of us who brought it from home. As the mother in Freud, Spanish was certissima. My parents admired this pedagogical system, not just because of the clear-cut division of linguistic time and space but because English was taught to students in the morning, "when their minds are fresher." They scolded me, scolded us, my sister and me, if we mixed. Our home mimicked the lines drawn by the family romance: Spanish with the mother, English with the father. A mixture of both (when nobody heard us) between sisters, a private language of sorts. I recognized that very same mixture not too long ago, in Buenos Aires, in a shop selling artesanías and indigenous art. Two well-dressed women, roughly my age, are fingering some alpaca-wool scarves while speaking to each other: "This one will look good on him, no te parece, but it's quite expensive, che, no quiero gastar tanto, después de todo, I don't know him that well." The switching is effortless: it may have its rules but I, as a speaker, am unaware of them, I can switch pero no puedo analizar. I tell myself: These women must have gone to the same school I did, and now that their parents are not around, they mix.

MIX

As I write, another linguistic detour comes to mind. In Argentina people don't say (or didn't use to say: like everything else, bilingualism has its fashions) bufanda, scarf; they said écharpe, or rather écharpé, sounding the final *e*. But the upper classes of course said écharpe, in impeccable French, which is the other language of Argentine culture. This is not so much bilingualism as a bilingual effect, not the work of switching but the work of citation, so typical of Argentines. Here, a cultural anecdote: José Bianco, admirable Argentine writer and editor of *Sur*, the review founded by Victoria Ocampo, was invited to lecture at Princeton. Distinguished Hispanists asked him what contact, if any, had he had with Américo Castro, the Spanish philosopher who spent years in exile in Buenos Aires before coming to the United States. What did Castro do in Argentina, these Hispanists, many of whom had been Castro's students at Princeton, wanted to know, whom did he converse with, how was he? Bianco: "He was very pleasant, charming, and he spoke like a posh Argentine woman." How could this be, wondered the flustered Hispanists, what on earth did Bianco mean? "Well, for every three words in Spanish he calculatingly dropped two in French, which, I must tell you, he spoke extremely well,"

Bianco answered quite casually. The conversation ended in general bewilderment: For these Hispanists, so intent on speaking and teaching "pure" Castilian Spanish, it was hard to accept that Castro would dare mix. Why wouldn't he, I wondered, since he championed heterodoxy?

PERFORMANCE

During childhood birthday parties, my sister and I were often called upon by our cousins on our mother's side, the mono-lingual one, to perform our bilingualism. It was both a show and a test: "Digan algo en inglés," they begged. My sister and I would say nothing, and the plea turned into a challenge: "We dare you to say something in English." Finally, as if plunging into water, one of us said to the other: "These kids are stupid idiots and we can say anything we like because they don't understand," or something to that effect. Our cousins then wanted us to translate what we had just said, "Qué dijeron, qué dijeron?" and when we said nothing and stood our ground, they got nasty. Only the announcement that the birthday cake was ready or that we were about to play a wonderful game would put a stop to the face-off.

Most of those cousins went on to learn English and a cou-ple moved to English-speaking countries. Which does not mean that they have forgotten those linguistic encounters.

PUNCTUM

Why do I speak of bilingualism, of my bilingualism, in only one language, and why am I doing it right now in English? An earlier version of this text was in Spanish: it came more naturally at the time, I don't exactly know why. Another question: how do you translate bilingualism, how do you convert the switching so that the effect of two languages working on each other, against each other, remains? Unavoidably, one must always be bilingual from one language, the heimlich one, if only for a moment, since "heim" or home can change: let's say one is bilingual from the language one settles into first, if only temporarily—the language of fleeting self-recognition.

This does not mean the language in which one feels more at ease, or the language one speaks the best, much less the language one has chosen to write in. There is (rather, one chooses) a point of support, and from that point one establishes a relation with the other language as absence, or rather as shadow, the object of linguistic desire. Although she has two languages, the bilingual subject always speaks as if she were lacking something, in a permanent state of need. (I think of this last phrase in French: "état de besoin." Among other things, the expression describes the state of an addict in need of a fix.)

ANIMAL TALK

What language do I use to speak to my pets? a friend wants to know. Never in French, I shoot right back, sure of myself. Maybe because French never quite became a home language for me, and animals are very much part of the home. I think some more and add that maybe I speak in English because I like speaking nonsense to them and call them silly names when no one is around, and nonsense comes naturally in English. But no, that's not quite the case, I add, I must talk to them in both English and Spanish because I often call the dog "mamita linda," and as you can well imagine, I never called anyone in my life "pretty mama," I wouldn't be caught dead, but with animals one can afford to be cute or "cursi," whatever. As for speaking nonsense, I guess it's not just limited to English because I used to call one of my hens, for quite some time, Curuzú Cuatiá. Don't ask me why: it's the Indian name of a town in an Argentine province, yet it sounded just right and made me cackle. Yes, I do speak Spanish to my chickens, I conclude without hesitation, and see the surprise in my friend's eyes. He did not know I had chickens. They come running to me when I call out, "Chicas, a comer!" and when I put them to bed at night I sing, "A la cama, a la cama, a la cama con Porcel" as they march into their coop. This I say as if confessing a serious sin; I who was never a fan of Jorge Porcel, one of the most vulgar and sexist entertainers in the history of Argentine television who did, indeed, invite young women to bed. My friend laughs and—I think—understands. But then, do they know about Porcel in Puerto Rico?

ECHOLALIAS

I increasingly find myself repeating inane phrases, little bits of half-forgotten speeches stored in my brain, absurd sayings derived from commonplace experiences that have remained in my memory, songs that I vaguely remember, or words that my sister and I invented when we were young, made up of languages we knew, languages we invented, and quotes learned by heart like "Un songe, devrais-je m'inquiéter d'un songe." All this becomes a drift that I repeat to myself when I'm alone; I wouldn't want anyone to hear me, they would think I'm losing my mind.

I recall that the father of a friend of mine, who was losing his, used to wander around the house repeating the word *Vatican*—it was the time of the Second Vatican Council—but pronouncing it in his maternal language. The *v* became a *p*, and his *Patican* greatly amused his audience until they got fed up. I also think of a friend who has lost most of her memory and who once in a while, in a voice so gruff she seems to have forgotten how to speak, suddenly bursts out with crazy sounds like "coochie coochie." I think of myself, of the times I catch myself muttering not exactly nonsense but small bits and pieces of the country I left behind, like the name of an indigenous insect, "mamboretá," or an inane ditty promoting a pain killer, "Mejor mejora Mejoral."

I wonder which language I'll speak in my dotage, if I reach that point, and in which language I'll die. Will I continue to be trilingual or will no one language lord it over the others in whatever comes out of my mouth?

I'm greatly relieved that, for once, it will not be up to me to make the choice.

PICTURES OF HOME

According to a piece published not too long ago in the *New York Times*, Chinese immigrants residing in the United States tend to speak English more fluently when they're shown images of some emblematic US landscape—Mount Rushmore, for example—and not of a Chinese one (say the Great Wall). In addition, when those who participated in this study were shown a photograph of a Chinese person and were asked to speak to that person in English, they were by far less loquacious than when shown the photograph of a US subject. The authors of this study described the experience as a case of frame switching and proposed that it was the brain's natural reaction to adapt to new frames of reference. The title of the piece in the *Times* summarized the experience: "Seeing Pictures of Home Can Make It Harder to Speak a Foreign Language."

In order to feel comfortable, even chatty in the other language, the piece seemed to conclude, total immersion in the foreign and oblivion of all the rest are needed: no trace must remain of the "home" left behind. But what if you carry that home with you? Or when foreignness has become an integral part of yourself?

One more thing: the piece in the *Times* does not stop to consider whom I speak to. To an other? To myself? To the image I am being shown?

FREEDOMS

In New York City street fairs, there are usually several stalls manned by Latin Americans, generally Indians from Andean regions. They sell clothing made of llama or alpaca wool, caps, some pottery, thick linen shirts. A friend tells me that a woman who works in the Peruvian consulate in New York is annoyed by these immigrants, perhaps because they are all too visible, but mainly for linguistic reasons. To be precise, she is irritated by a bilingualism over which, as a representative of the government of her country, she has no control. "These people go directly from Quechua to English," she complains in aggrieved tones.

SPEAKING FROM DIFFERENT PLACES

To be bilingual is to speak being fully aware that what is being said is always being said in another place, in many other places. This awareness of the inherent strangeness of all communication, this knowing that what is being said is always necessarily alien, that speaking always implies insufficiency and above all else doubling, if not duplicity (there is always another way of saying it), is applicable to any language in itself, but in our need for transparency and contact, we tend to forget it. The explicit, often messy bilingualism of the subject wielding more than one language—through a habit or laziness, as a provocation, for aesthetic needs, sometimes simultaneously, sometimes sequentially—renders that otherness patent. That is the bilingual subject's privilege; it is also her undoing. I recall what Nabokov says of his passage to English: in translating *Despair*, he discovers he can use English as "a wistful standby" for Russian. Replacing one language for another is not devoid of melancholy: "I still feel the pangs of that substitution." I also remember that, many years ago, before I left Argentina, I found a memorable phrase in a text by Valery Larbaud. In a list of recommendations to potential writers, he advised them to "donner un air étranger a ce qu'on écrit." The advice struck me as brilliant:

it turned what I considered a fault into an advantage, uncomfortable to be sure but an advantage nonetheless. It gave me permission to write "in translation." And so I did, and continue to do so.

IMMIGRANT BILINGUALISM

José Ramirez Salguero is from El Salvador and has been living in the United States for some time. He is not a permanent immigrant but something like a legal guest, one who is allowed to work in the US and return, every so often, to his country of origin. He is somewhat bilingual, that is to say he manages pretty well in a fluid, somewhat macaronic English, and his eyes light up when he realizes that the person he is talking to speaks Spanish.

José Ramírez Salguero has started a building company that employs all his younger brothers, who are also called José, but can be told apart by their second name: José Elías, José Ramón, José David. Other men from El Salvador also work there, one of them, with very blue eyes, is called Bartleby, like Melville's character, and I will never know the reason for his name. I don't dare ask; he would answer that he prefers not to tell me. Unlike his literary namesake, however, he is a very energetic and enthusiastic workman, one who, like the original José, is living out his American dream.

If José is somewhat bilingual, his brothers and colleagues are less so. This has given rise to a language in between, in which syntax follows the rules of Spanish but technical words, in particular those relating to the building industry which are not familiar to Salvadorean ears, are kept in English or something that sounds like English. So it is that a martillo or a taladro coexist with the shirra, which I soon learned was sheetrock; that we speak of the rufo and the bes-men; and that the word caldera, which I once used instead of boila, was met with blank stares. They must use another word in El Salvador, so I make do with boila, and with shirra, and we get along fine. In a country that is not our own, that's the most important.

BILINGUAL CROSSINGS

In a deranged attempt to clean the country of undesirables, the Dominican dictator Rafael Leónidas Trujillo decided in 1937 to do away with the Haitians who crossed the border on a daily basis looking for work or those who had crossed it years earlier to settle in a country offering them better opportunities. The control to which the presumed Haitians had to submit was purely linguistic. The subject was stopped at the border, asked to pronounce the word perejil or, according to others, tijera colorada, and if they pronounced it with a guttural *rrr*, as in their native French, or pronounced the hard-to-utter Spanish *j* with a guttural gasp, they were not allowed to enter the country and, in more than one case, was killed. Perejil—parsley in Spanish—worked here like a shibboleth, as with the members of the tribe of Ephraim: it revealed an intolerable foreignness, a non-belonging. It is said that between fifteen and twenty thousand persons died in this way, among them many Haitians who, although pronouncing the Spanish letter *j* correctly, were darker-skinned.

The name of the river marking the border between the two countries was called—and may still be called—Massacre, in remembrance of the violence that took place there many years before these sinister crossings. The name is pronounced the same in French and Spanish. Except, of course, for that telltale *rrr* that sounds like a growl.

NAME

What name does one give the bilingual subject, the newly born for whom one foresees a bilingual life? I have often heard future parents say that they want a name that will work in both languages, with minimal adaptation, without any need for translation. Let us say Tomás / Thomas, or Olivia / Olivia, or Ana / Anna, or Martín / Martin. (No Hermenegildos, please, no Duncans, no Jesuses, no Socorros.) There may be something to the passepartout names that may make life easier for the child who navigates between cultures. But, in more general terms, no name works "in both languages"; there is always a need for translation. The same may be said of surnames. Mine is unquestionably Irish to British, Irish, or American ears. But in Argentina, where it is often pronounced with a stress on the first syllable, more than once it has been thought Jewish: If Portnoy, why not Mólloy? And during a trip through Burgundy, years ago, it was considered "un nom du pays": indeed, there is a little village close to Dijon named Moloy.

BY ANY OTHER NAME

Her name was Ana María but one of my aunts on my father's side started calling her Annie May, perhaps because she found her given name too Argentine. The nickname remained, even replaced the original, but was hispanized immediately. Both my mother and my aunt, who only spoke Spanish, pronounced it (and even wrote it) Animé and only called her Ana María when they scolded her or wanted her to pay attention. I should add that Japanese animation did not yet exist in those days and my sister had no way of knowing that her nickname, now become her name, would one day signify a cartoon.

There was never any problem with my name. But that is not entirely true: I am Sylvia, with a *y*, as it is in English, and that was enough in those days to render me foreign, or at least different. It was also enough to have it misspelled every time I gave it, which caused endless bureaucratic problems in a country fixated on accurate documentation.

My parents used to say that they had given both my sister and me only one given name to make life less complicated. They were wrong: for a bilingual person, complication is life itself and it usually starts with a name.

BILINGUAL BINGES

I think of the pleasure of recovering a language, of plunging into it without giving a thought, for one short moment, to the others you usually speak. For a moment you indulge yourself, you pretend you're monolingual, you revel in the many possibilities of this only language you master so well.

Yesterday I was on the telephone with a friend in Paris with whom I had not spoken for some time. We did email each other, which for me meant sending her messages in impeccable French, a tedious task at best since accents, cedillas, and circumflexes slowed down my pace. But this time I just had to speak to her on the phone and enjoyed doing so, giving in to the vocal luxury of the other language, the one I don't usually speak. I did so as a nouveau riche who suddenly realizes the extent of her unexpected fortune, with showy displays of adverbial clauses, lots of quand meme, tout compte fait, and par surcroit. I considered slipping in a qu'a cela ne tienne, but then I thought it was going too far. When I hung up and went to the other room, I realized that the electrician who was repairing an outlet there had been listening, had recognized I was speaking French, and was impressed by my plurilingualism. He himself is Polish, finds it hard to speak English, and we often communicate through

gestures. While leaving, he pointed at something he was seeing through the window and, with a big smile, said a word
that sounded like a combination of *deers* and *bears*, a word I
did not understand. After several attempts at repeating what
he had said, with considerable embarrassment on both sides,
I approached the window and realized he was not speaking
of deer or bears at all but trying to pronounce the word *birds*
in English. It was his attempt to speak another language the
way I had done on the phone, in a carefree, happy way—
after all a bird in hand is well worth a qu'a cela ne tienne on
the phone—and I, full of myself and my self-conscious performance in French, had not even guessed at what he was
saying. I felt very guilty.

LAPSUS

In what language does one wake up? When I'm away from home, traveling, and the phone rings, I answer half-asleep, making an effort to do so in the right language, the language spoken there. If I don't, I feel I've made a bad blunder, I've been careless, have been caught off guard. I've allowed something that usually remains unseen to be seen—although I don't quite know what that is. It's as if I had been surprised in a compromising position. One morning, still half-asleep, I started speaking to the woman lying next to me and she seemed not to understand me. She just smiled while I kept repeating my words, exasperated at her failure to understand me. It was like one of those dreams in which you think you're saying something but the words never come out of your mouth. Suddenly I woke up completely and realized that I had been speaking to her in the other language, the language she did not know. I never found out what it was that I really wanted to tell her. And why do I say "really"?

RECOGNITION

Surprisingly my friend who suffers from Alzheimer's has not forgotten her English, which she learned in her youth. She simply no longer knows how to use it. Let me explain: if someone says something to her in English, she answers in perfect English. If someone speaks to her in Spanish, the same thing happens. But if during a conversation in Spanish someone switches languages, she gets completely flustered. She can no longer switch back and forth like a regular bilingual, she remains attached to the language in which the conversation began, trying in vain to understand from Spanish what is now being said in English.

The last time this happened she panicked, I saw it in her eyes, as if a stranger had walked into the room. I wonder if the same thing would happen if a conversation in English switched without warning to Spanish. Would she try to understand what was being said from English or would she simply adjust? I suspect she'd recognize the intruder and remain unfazed, but in reality I have no basis to support this, just a vague belief in the resilience of the so-called mother tongue.

But if the illness does not allow her to recognize her people, how would she recognize her language, which would feel alienated, perhaps threatening?

VIOLENCE

Jules Supervielle, a Franco-Uruguayan bilingual and a French poet, believed that you could only write in one language: Choosing to become a French poet, he decided to "délibérément ferme[r] à l'espagnol mes portes secrètes, celles qui ouvrent sur la pensée, l'expression et, disons, l'âme." Spanish for him was a remnant, bits and pieces, "borborygmes de langage." Borborygme, it will be remembered, is the gurgle caused by flatulence. We're talking here of linguistic burps or farts. Supervielle's niece, also a writer, tells me that Supervielle had imposed French-only at home and that his wife Pilar, like him a native Uruguayan, found it immensely hard to speak French, "to the point that it was painful to listen to her," says Silvia Baron Supervielle, "she seemed to be doing so much violence to herself, she was another person." The husband's Spanish burps had been replaced by the wife's French ones. What price poetry. This niece of Supervielle also writes, poetry in particular. She doesn't want to be considered solely a poet. She's a writer, she says. And, moreover, a translator.

ACCENT

Alan Pauls recalls how, as a child in Buenos Aires, he envied foreign singers who sang in Spanish with an accent: Ornella Vanoni, Nicola di Bari, Domenico Modugno—a list to which I must of course add Vikki Carr's memorably weird "Y volveré." As for myself, I remember how my sister and I, listening to the radio, relished the oddly accented and probably barely understood English of the memorable Lillian Red, née Nélida Esther Corriale, lady crooner for the band Héctor y Su Gran Orquesta de Jazz, who sang that she loved somebody with all her hadansoul. I took me some time to realize that hadansoul was heart and soul. Hadansoul seemed so much more mysterious, like an Oriental potion of some sort, sexy, perhaps obscene, to the child I was then.

I never spoke with an accent, by which I mean an accent that would show that I was passing from one language to another. Even though I make this a point of honor, in memory of the good student I once thought myself to be, a part of me regrets it. As a child, I remember imitating my English-speaking aunts and calling the neighborhood they lived in "Belgraahno" until a non-English-speaking aunt on my mother's side stopped me short, told me I was speaking pidgin Spanish, and that I should pronounce the name Belgrano correctly. He was, after all, a founding father.

To speak with an accent betrays the speaker: he or she is not from here. Sometimes the speaker comes from somewhere prestigious, speaks Spanish with a French accent or English with a British one. But this is not always the case. A few months after I came to the United States speaking my somewhat outdated, Anglo-Argentine English, the only one I knew, I was placed not by the shores of the Thames but much farther away: "Are you from India?" someone asked politely in a department store in Buffalo, New York. For some reason the distant colonial reference vexed me although it was, in a funny way, accurate: I was not quite the English girl I thought myself to be.

TONGUE AND TRAUMA

Can one speak of trauma in the language one once spoke—better said, in the language in which one was—at the very moment that trauma occurs? I think of Elie Wiesel who, before Auschwitz, spoke several languages. After Auschwitz, he devoted himself to the study of a new language, French, which he saw as a necessary challenge, and in it, defiantly, wrote his remaining work. "I wanted to demonstrate that I had entered another period, wanted to prove to myself that I was alive, that I had survived. I wanted to continue being who I was but in another setting." As I read this, I remember thinking: to say the unsayable Wiesel needs, above all, to destabilize the ease with which he spoke the other languages.

I think of Olga Bernal, who also changed her linguistic landscape, possibly for the same reasons. She went first from Czech to French in order to write her essays and then, towards the end of her life, when for some reason she felt summoned to testify to the trauma of Auschwitz, she changed once more. French had become for her too comfortable.

Better said, she changed her means of expression: she abandoned literature for sculpture.

THE FATHER TONGUE

The dream of the severed tongue, seeped in red, returns nearly every night: the Bulgarian maid's lover, brandishing a knife very close to the child's face, threatens to cut out his tongue if he tells on them. What language do they speak? The man can only threaten in Bulgarian, the boy, in order to denounce the lovers, would have to do so in Ladino, the language he shares with his parents. For even as a child, Elias Canetti speaks many languages: Bulgarian for the outside world, Ladino for the family, English with his father (when the family moves to London), German, much later, with his mother. Or he speaks none.

Ladino is the language for the familiar, but it is not the language the parents speak between themselves. The couple's intimacy takes place in German, a language literally forbidden to the son. "I was not allowed to understand it." His parents refuse to include him in their dialogue: "After begging them in vain I would shut myself up in a room that was rarely used and repeated the words I had heard them utter to myself, using the same tone, as if they were magic formulas." He is always careful that his parents did not find him doing this: if they have their secrets, he has his own.

When his father dies, his mother subjects him to a brutal acquisition of German, has him memorize phrases from a book he is never allowed to see, and scolds him viciously when he makes a mistake. The boy finally does learn, and the mother proudly recognizes herself in this linguistic success: "You are my son, after all."

ESCRITURAS

In terms of writing, how and by what means does the bilingual subject enter language? The Cuban slave Juan Francisco
Manzano (of whom it could be said that he worked in two
languages, his own hybrid Spanish and the Spanish of his
master) learns to write by literally tracing the writing of the
other. That second language—nineteenth-century literary
Spanish—will become his own for poetry, yet when he writes
down his life, at his master's bidding, he goes back to his
other Spanish, the messy one.

I remember similar exercises in mimesis. When I wrote
my first book in French, I tried to imitate the writing of my
dissertation adviser, paying close attention to the idioms that
peppered his discourse: for example, qu'à cela ne tienne.
When I wrote my first texts in Spanish, I filtered—the verb is
not excessive—everything I wanted to say through my readings of Borges. When I wrote my first book in English, I
trained for the exercise like an athlete. Until then, English was
a practical language, destined for the everyday life of exile,
but also the language of affections, past and present. And it
was the language of memory: the memory of my father. In
order to regain ease in written English—ease and authority—

I did not follow prestigious examples but practiced a bric-à-brac effect. I would write words on bits of paper, expressions, clauses (usually adversatives) that I liked and wished to use, a little as if I were plagiarizing. It was an adventure in translation.

I have written the key word: translation. I will not dwell on its implications, just mark its power for the bilingual subject as a permanent reminder of that "being in between" that marks our speech, our writing, our tenuous life. And while on the subject of translation, one last anecdote. Years ago, back in Argentina after many years spent in France and before I attempted to write anything of my own in Spanish, I entered two translation contests together with a friend. One was a translation from French to Spanish (Jean Paulhan), the other from English to Spanish (Virginia Woolf). When we were done (it was a collaborative venture), we had to choose a pseudonym. My friend always claimed that I got depressed when I translated, I was so gloomy, she said, qué cara de tormenta, che. For my part, I had just finished reading *Tropic of Cancer* and treasured the scene in the Paris bordello where Miller's friend, the Indian Nanantatee, defecated in the bidet because he had no idea what a bidet was for: It was a culturally alien artifact. My friend and I chose Gloomy Nonentity for a pseudonym. We won both prizes. Today, I would certainly not use that adjective to qualify the task of the translator or the life of the bilingual subject and would look for something more upbeat. I would, however, keep the noun.

ONE OR THE OTHER BUT NOT BOTH

Those who hear a bilingual person speak fluently in an acquired language are not always aware that the person is also fluent in another. When they find out, the person is considered somewhat of an impostor, even—why not?—a traitor. This perception is shared to a certain extent by bilingual subjects themselves. They conceal that other, first language that would betray them, working to keep it secret, and if they find themselves having to utter a word in it, they often do so with a slight accent so that no one will think they have passed to the other side.

But flitting from language to language has its price and not all switchings are equal. Take the brilliant, all-but-forgotten Calvert Casey, author of the appropriately titled *Notes from a Simulator*. His works often bear titles that allude to displacement: "The Walk," "El Paseo," "El Regreso," "In Partenza." His very life is a permanent to-and-fro: born in the US to an American father and a Cuban mother, he writes his first story in English and wins a prize, leaves for Cuba where he writes in Spanish and becomes a Cuban writer, then goes from Cuba to Europe where he works as an interpreter, settles down in Rome, writes his last novel in English, destroys it save for one chapter in which he narrates an excursion—an identity-erasing drift, really—within the labyrinth of his lover's body. Then he commits suicide.

One could say that Casey was an American writer at the beginning, when he wrote in English. He then put that language in storage during the better part of his life and only at the very end returned to it and, in a sense, lost his life to it. In between he was a Cuban writer writing in Spanish.

His friends say he stuttered, like the protagonist in his story "El regreso," and that at times he would remain speechless, his mouth open, his tongue not moving. Maybe, like one of his characters, he spoke "with a vague foreign accent." But in which language—or rather from which language—was that foreignness perceived? And most importantly: In which language does the stutter occur?

One last detail haunts me: Calvert Casey, who was often called La Calvita, or Baldie, killed himself by taking an overdose. This much I know. But every time I think of his death in Rome, I imagine him jumping out a window from the highest floor of a building onto the courtyard below, as if he needed to finally land.

I cannot get rid of that image.

TITLES

I have just finished a novel in Spanish, a novel about, among other things, bilingualism and displacement, about the impossibility of being in only one space, only one language. When it came time to find a title, I couldn't think of one, that is, I couldn't think of a title in Spanish that might reflect or in some way allude to what I had written. When I tried to distance myself from the novel, the distance I needed to name it, Spanish failed me. I only found distance through a change of language, and indeed it was in English that the first title came to me, a title paradoxically stressing the homey feeling the novel sought to dispel: *Back Home*. I ran this title past several friends, most of whom found it too curt; but I liked its noncommittal terseness, whereas nothing in Spanish convinced me. So I sent away my novel to my Argentine publisher with its temporary English title: *Back Home* (título provisorio). For weeks I mulled over possible titles in Spanish but nothing I came up with met anyone's approval, including my own. Then I understood that only a quotation would give me the distancing effect that the temporary title in English had helped achieve. In leafing through Borges, I found at random a phrase I liked, "El común olvido," which won me over immediately. I truly cannot say where, in Borges, I found it; it was a chance quotation. Then, with the Spanish title in place, I revisited the English "Back Home" and found I could do better, not through literal translation but by a kind of linguistic derivation. So I scrapped "Back Home" and decided that my novel, in its yet-to-come English form, would be titled *All but Forgotten*; not a translation, not even a quotation, but the product of many goings back and forth between languages, which amounts to the same. The two titles do not mean the same thing, I know; yet for me they are equal, in the sense that they determine one another, make no sense independently.

MES APPRENTISSAGES

I have dwelled on this shuttling between languages because it is the very stuff of my writing. It is often exhilarating, liberating; it is also laborious, fatiguing. I grew up trilingual, or very nearly trilingual. Spanish was my first language; English followed soon thereafter, when I was three and a half; French, when I was about eight. Because the three languages were learned in succession and not simultaneously, they came to occupy different spaces and each took on an affect of its own. This was reinforced by the fact that my sister and I were trained (both at home and in our bilingual school) to keep the languages separate. At the Anglo-Argentine school we were sent to, there was a time for each language: English in the morning, Spanish in the afternoon, and never the twain, etc. If one was caught speaking Spanish during the English period, one was severely punished. And yet we indulged in what seemed like a terribly attractive transgression, resorting to the forbidden language during breaks, a Spanish we would whisper for fear that some zealous teacher might overhear us and march us into the Head's office. Interestingly, dirty jokes were told in Spanish; or rather, the general gist of the joke was told in English, but body parts deemed unmentionable were named in Spanish, much in the way nineteenth-century medical texts named them in Latin. I only learned their equivalent in English through my readings: another profitable use of literature.

French came later in my childhood, and by personal choice. Whereas Spanish and English came "naturally" as part of my family romance—I spoke Spanish with my mother, English with my father—French resulted from my own initiative. French was the language of my mother's family yet she herself did not speak it. I wanted to recover it for her sake, didn't want my father to be bilingual and not my mother. So a French teacher was found, an old friend of one of my mother's aunts who came to us every Saturday and quite despaired when, not knowing a word in French, my sister and I resolutely Frenchified its Spanish equivalent. Madame Suzanne, as she was called, wore turbans, and had us listen to Charles Trenet. When I hear "Ménilmontant," I inevitably recall my parents' dining room, Madame Suzanne, my sister and I around the Victrola, my mother hovering in the adjoining living room as if she wanted to join us. When I hear "Ménilmontant," it makes me a little sad, then it irritates me: once heard, I cannot get it out of my head.

SAVOIR FAIRE

To each language its own. As a child, I wrote moralizing little stories in Spanish, much to my aunt's delight: I was a good, principled child. I wrote essays in English at school and got middling grades; "no imagination" was the curt remark at the top of my papers. Then I decided to be funny in English, sassy. I changed my tone; the teacher read my essays out loud to the class, everybody laughed, and my grades went up. I realized I could be funny in English in a way that I could not in Spanish, I realized too that humor was not without danger: "I don't know how the board examiners will react to this," my English teacher warned. I was funny at my own expense.

I did not write in French until much later, and then I did not just write little papers, I wrote about "literature." It was a more complex experience, a sentimental education—another story.

EL CIELO DE PARIS

Happy to see my enthusiasm for French, my mother sent me to the Alliance Française to study literature. It was more than we did at school in English, where literature meant either memorizing Shakespeare or struggling through Thomas Hardy. I was thirteen or fourteen when I plunged into the foreign realm of French literature, taught by a Frenchwoman under whose spell I immediately succumbed. I studied her reactions closely, learned to prefer Racine's passion to Corneille's duty (two feelings I was barely familiar with), to find Bossuet tedious and La Rochefoucauld acute, to say "Victor Hugo, hélas!" and love Baudelaire, adore Flaubert, take it upon myself to prefer *L'éducation sentimentale*, just because my teacher claimed to prefer it to *Madame Bovary*. I loved what she loved, or what I thought she loved. I still do (with the exception of *L'éducation sentimentale* which I do not prefer to *Madame Bovary*). Yet when I wrote my first novel, many, many years later, remembering that French teacher, how much I worshipped her, and how she seemed to gently mock my adoration, I adapted a scene of *L'éducation* to my own needs, the scene where an aging Madame Arnoux returns to see Frédéric one last time, hoping, in vain, to reawaken his love for her. Mimicry is, after all, one of the finest forms of sincerity.

ALTERATION

One always writes from an absence, the choice of a language automatically signifying the postponement of another. What at first would seem an imposition—why does one have to choose?—quickly turns into an advantage. The absence of what is postponed continues to work, obscurely, on the chosen language, suffusing it, even better, contaminating it, with an autrement dit that brings it unexpected eloquence. That alterity, or alteration, also disturbs the reading habits of the bilingual subject. I know that when I drive on a highway and see a sign saying "Icy Pavement," for a split second I inevitably think icy as if it were in French (and medieval French to boot). Or when I drive down a country road and see the sign "Hay," my first reaction is to read it in Spanish—hay: there is, or we have—and wonder what it is they have to sell, before realizing that it is . . . hay. For me, the sign should read, hay hay, the first in Spanish, the second in English. I find these trivial little miscomprehensions annoying yet cannot avoid them; I am always caught, for a second, off guard.

I wrote the word alterity which brings to my mind the French for satisfying one's thirst, désaltérer. The writing of a bilingual writer, I would venture, is out of need always altered, never "disaltered"; always thirsty, always wanting, never satisfied. And it is also, in another sense, alterada, in the way I used to hear the Spanish term used by my mother, my aunts, when referring to somebody who was slightly off, who could not control her thoughts, her voice.

FAUX PAS

They say that Jules Supervielle would get very upset, even furious, when he discovered that an expression, a turn of phrase, even a word inadvertently used in a poem, betrayed the Spanish behind his French. He could not bear contamination, linguistic crossbreeding; he had chosen once and for all, even forced his whole family to speak French and only French. While not afraid of mixture, I too am not immune to linguistic embarrassment. When I travel, back to Buenos Aires, say, or back to Paris, I worry that, distracted or half-asleep, I will answer the telephone in one of the other languages, the wrong one. Why would this language be wrong, be a source of shame? I don't know, but it is as if I were guilty of something, caught unprepared, in a compromising position.

THE WRITING LESSON

To go from one language to another, as from one activity to another, requires practice. Since I went to university in France, I was used to thinking about literature in French. Spanish had remained behind, in Argentina. Also English, which had become for me a practical language, the language of travel, not of literature; also the language in which I wrote, on occasion, to my father. I remember the day, while in Paris, when I was asked to do a book review for a French/Latin American journal in Spanish. It was like forced labor. A beginner, I found neither the tone, or rather the intonation, as Borges would have put it, to say what I wanted to say; indeed, I didn't even quite know what I wanted to say. The change of language had literally disarmed me, I who felt quite comfortable doing book reports in French. I felt I could say one thing just as well as its opposite, provided it sounded good. I was an impostor desperate not to be caught. Finally, I remember standing one morning, in desperation, at the exit of the Luxembourg metro station, hoping to catch an Argentine friend who, I knew, attended a seminar at the Sorbonne at ten o'clock. As soon as I saw her coming up the stairs, I felt relieved. I accompanied her to her class, showering her with questions, endowing her with an authority over language that, when it came to writing, I lacked: "Can you write such and such in Spanish?" "Does this phrase sound right to you?" "Is it awkward to put an adverb at the beginning of a sentence?" "Does this sound translated?" And so it went, on and on, the two of us walking down Boulevard Saint-Michel, I receiving my first lesson in critical writing in what was my mother tongue from a woman who obviously had more important things on her mind than my linguistic insecurity.

More than once I have glanced at the book review that resulted from such anguish, my first published piece. The effort is obvious. The article is well informed, clear, boring: a lesson in mediocre writing. My "real" written Spanish would come later, after reading Borges, and even then, for a long time, I wrote only criticism, I would not allow myself to write fiction in any sustained way. I did write fragments, a little guiltily, perhaps, in all three languages; recollections, scenes, sometimes a quote from what I was reading, a turn of phrase, an inane parody ("Yes, Julia, there was a tiger. But that was not the point"), with the notion that these notes might come in handy someday. I did indeed use many of these fragments much later, in the writing of *Certificate of Absence*.

When I decided to teach myself to write critical prose in English, the exercise was different. I readied myself for the task like an athlete preparing for a competition. I could not resort to sassiness, which had worked so well during my adolescence, so I wrote down words, expressions, adverbial clauses that I heard or read and thought I might want to use, a little as if I were getting ready to plagiarize: notwithstanding, hitherto, despite, unequivocally, conversely. That I chose to write the book I did in English was probably not accidental, although I know I did not plan it. It was a book on autobiography, and writing it in English was, in a sense, a way of remembering my father.

ORIGINAL TEXT

Years ago, I taught a freshman honors seminar on "Story-telling" that was both an introduction to Latin American literature and a reflection on the crisscrossing of languages. The texts we worked with were by Borges, whom few of the students had read.

Most of the students were, in fact, bilingual. Not Spanish–English bilingual, as one might have expected, but bilingual in another language, one that most of them seemed to leave at home and did not particularly want to revive. At home they spoke Chinese, Hungarian, Arabic, Hindi, with their parents and, perhaps, with some elderly relative they helped take care of. The so-called heritage language seemed in fact to have disinherited them; or they had disinherited it.

While reading Borges's fiction went relatively smoothly, reading his poems became unexpectedly complex. The edition of the poetry we used had the original poems in Spanish on the pages to the left and the English version, facing them, on the pages to the right. On the one hand, this seemed reassuring: yes, there was an original text. On the other, it caused discomfort: the readers had two texts facing each other, facing off, as it were, and had to remind themselves the text on the left was the original and the text on the right its translation and not, as some of them expected, the opposite. "How do I know what I'm reading?" was an often-heard complaint.

I have often asked myself whether the fact that this course began barely a week after the attack on the Twin Towers—an event which literally dislocated so many of us in time, in space, and, one might say. in nation—had something to do with the students' reaction. For one moment we were all New Yorkers, we were all from here, we all spoke English as a first language.

Even I fell into the trap: a few days after the attack, when classes were about to begin, I looked through the list of students that had signed up for my class and saw a name that was unmistakably Arab. I worried that this might spur some confrontation in the classroom: a hijab that would be impossible to ignore, a cultural conflict that I would not quite know how to handle. On the first day of class, as I called the roll for the first time, I identified the student in question: she turned out to be a queer young woman, with strands of hair dyed bright blue and a pierced nostril. I was relieved that here was a difference I knew how to translate.

MEMORY

To clarify things (not to simplify them), let me say that, at this point in my life, I write fiction in Spanish (and cannot imagine doing otherwise); criticism in English and Spanish (and, on occasion, in French); that I read fiction mainly in English; that the poems I remember by heart are in French; that I like to translate Spanish texts into English, and English texts into Spanish, including my own, which improve with this shuttling; and that the quotations that my memory brings up now and then, bits of texts, like relics, that come to me for no good reason ("Un songe, me devrais-je inquiéter d'un songe") are in French and Spanish, rarely in English, except for the occasional Shakespeare: "And all for use of that which is my own." If I were to lose my memory, I ask myself, what will my mind retain from that archive? A friend of mine cannot remember what she has been told an hour before and fails to recognize people she hasn't seen for a while, yet she can recite, without hesitation, the beginning of Aristophanes' *The Frogs* in Greek, learned in adolescence. Were I to lose my memory, what would I recite, I wonder?' In what language does memory speak, when the mind is shattered and reminiscence spent?

ABOUT THE AUTHOR

Sylvia Molloy was born in Argentina in 1938. Her father was born in Argentina of British parents and her mother was the youngest of eight children born to French parents. Molloy's entire life was lived "between" languages, national imaginaries, countries, and educational systems. Educated in Argentina and France where she received her PhD from the Sorbonne, she established a very distinguished career in the United States as the first woman to receive tenure at Princeton, then moving on to Yale before being accepted the Albert Schweitzer Chair of Humanities at New York University. Molloy was awarded several major fellowships from foundations such as the Guggenheim, National Endowment for the Humanities, the Social Science Research Council, and Civitella Ranieri (Italy). She served as president of the Modern Language Association of America in 2001 and the International Institute of Latin American Studies. Molloy's reputation as an outstanding thinker/writer also developed "between" academic and intellectual/artistic circles in the Americas and beyond. Her highly successful academic books—*La Diffusion de la littérature hispano-americanine en France au XXe siècle* (1972), *Las letras de Borges* (1979), *At Face Value: Autobiographical Writing in Spanish America* (1991), and *Hispanisms and Homosexualities* (with Robert McKee Irwin, 1998)—established her as one of the leading Hispanists and queer theorists in the United States while novels such as *En breve cárcel* (1981; *Certificate of Absence*, 1989) and *El común olvido* (2002) launched her as literary figure and "a queer-literature icon" in Latin America (Modern Language Association). Molloy's final writings were short prose pieces—*Varia imaginación* (2003) and *Vivir entre lenguas* (2016), *Desarticulaciones* (2010; *Dislocations*, 2022), and *Animalia* (2022).

Sylvia Molloy lived with her life partner, Emily Geiger, and their countless animals in New York and Argentina until her death in 2022.

ACKNOWLEDGMENTS

Diana Taylor and Emily Geiger would like to thank Richard Schechner and Bishan Samaddar for their support.